CS-3 GENERAL APTITUDE AND ABILITIES SERIES

This is your PASSBOOK for...

Administration, Management and Supervision

Test Preparation Study Guide
Questions & Answers

NLC®

NATIONAL LEARNING CORPORATION®

National Learning Corporation

212 Michael Drive, Syosset, NY 11791
(516) 921-8888 • www.passbooks.com
E-mail: info@passbooks.com

PUBLISHED IN THE UNITED STATES OF AMERICA

PASSBOOK® SERIES

THE *PASSBOOK® SERIES* has been created to prepare applicants and candidates for the ultimate academic battlefield – the examination room.

At some time in our lives, each and every one of us may be required to take an examination – for validation, matriculation, admission, qualification, registration, certification, or licensure.

Based on the assumption that every applicant or candidate has met the basic formal educational standards, has taken the required number of courses, and read the necessary texts, the *PASSBOOK® SERIES* furnishes the one special preparation which may assure passing with confidence, instead of failing with insecurity. Examination questions – together with answers – are furnished as the basic vehicle for study so that the mysteries of the examination and its compounding difficulties may be eliminated or diminished by a sure method.

This book is meant to help you pass your examination provided that you qualify and are serious in your objective.

The entire field is reviewed through the huge store of content information which is succinctly presented through a provocative and challenging approach – the question-and-answer method.

A climate of success is established by furnishing the correct answers at the end of each test.

You soon learn to recognize types of questions, forms of questions, and patterns of questioning. You may even begin to anticipate expected outcomes.

You perceive that many questions are repeated or adapted so that you can gain acute insights, which may enable you to score many sure points.

You learn how to confront new questions, or types of questions, and to attack them confidently and work out the correct answers.

You note objectives and emphases, and recognize pitfalls and dangers, so that you may make positive educational adjustments.

Moreover, you are kept fully informed in relation to new concepts, methods, practices, and directions in the field.

You discover that you are actually taking the examination all the time: you are preparing for the examination by "taking" an examination, not by reading extraneous and/or supererogatory textbooks.

In short, this PASSBOOK®, used directedly, should be an important factor in helping you to pass your test.

CIVIL SERVICE
ADMINISTRATION, MANAGEMENT AND SUPERVISION

OVERVIEW

Tests in administration, management and supervision form the backbone and integral portion of nearly all levels of civil service promotional exams. Study of this book is recommended to all those candidates where intensive preparation in this area is necessary or desired.

SUPERVISION

INTRODUCTION

These questions test for knowledge of the principles and practices employed in planning, organizing, and controlling the activities of a work unit toward predetermined objectives. The concepts covered, usually in a situational question format, include such topics as assigning and reviewing work; evaluating performance; maintaining work standards; motivating and developing subordinates; implementing procedural change; increasing efficiency; and dealing with problems of absenteeism, morale, and discipline.

Test Task: You will be presented with situations in which you must apply knowledge of the principles and practices of supervision in order to answer the questions correctly.

1. Assume that the unit you supervise is given a new work assignment and that you are unsure about the proper procedure to use in performing this assignment. Which one of the following actions should you take FIRST in this situation? 1.____
   A. Obtain input from your staff.
   B. Consult other unit supervisors who have had similar assignments.
   C. Use an appropriate procedure from a similar assignment that you are familiar with.
   D. Discuss the matter with your supervisor.

KEY (CORRECT ANSWERS)

1. The correct answer is D. This question asks for the action that you should take FIRST in this situation.
   Choice A is not correct. Since this assignment is new for your unit, your staff would not be expected to be more knowledgeable than you about the proper procedure.
   Choice B is not correct. Although discussing this matter with other supervisors may increase your knowledge of the new assignment, similar assignments performed in other units may differ in some important way from your new assignment. Other units may also function differently from your unit, so the procedures used to perform similar assignments may differ accordingly.
   Choice C is not correct. Since this assignment is new for your unit, you would have no way of knowing whether the procedure from a similar assignment is appropriate to use. You would need someone with the appropriate knowledge, usually your supervisor, to determine if the procedure from a similar assignment could be used before you actually employed this procedure in the performance of your new assignment.
   Choice D is the correct answer. Your supervisor is more likely to be informed about what procedure may be appropriate for work that he or she assigns to you than would other unit supervisors or your staff. Even if your supervisor dos not know what procedure is appropriate, a decision regarding which procedure to use should be made with his or her participation, since he or she has the ultimate responsibility for your unit's work.

HOW TO TAKE A TEST

You have studied long, hard and conscientiously.

With your official admission card in hand, and your heart pounding, you have been admitted to the examination room.

You note that there are several hundred other applicants in the examination room waiting to take the same test.

They all appear to be equally well prepared.

You know that nothing but your best effort will suffice. The "moment of truth" is at hand: you now have to demonstrate objectively, in writing, your knowledge of content and your understanding of subject matter.

You are fighting the most important battle of your life—to pass and/or score high on an examination which will determine your career and provide the economic basis for your livelihood.

What extra, special things should you know and should you do in taking the examination?

I. YOU MUST PASS AN EXAMINATION

A. WHAT EVERY CANDIDATE SHOULD KNOW

Examination applicants often ask us for help in preparing for the written test. What can I study in advance? What kinds of questions will be asked? How will the test be given? How will the papers be graded?

B. HOW ARE EXAMS DEVELOPED?

Examinations are carefully written by trained technicians who are specialists in the field known as "psychological measurement," in consultation with recognized authorities in the field of work that the test will cover. These experts recommend the subject matter areas or skills to be tested; only those knowledges or skills important to your success on the job are included. The most reliable books and source materials available are used as references. Together, the experts and technicians judge the difficulty level of the questions.

Test technicians know how to phrase questions so that the problem is clearly stated. Their ethics do not permit "trick" or "catch" questions. Questions may have been tried out on sample groups, or subjected to statistical analysis, to determine their usefulness.

Written tests are often used in combination with performance tests, ratings of training and experience, and oral interviews. All of these measures combine to form the best-known means of finding the right person for the right job.

II. HOW TO PASS THE WRITTEN TEST

A. BASIC STEPS

1) Study the announcement

How, then, can you know what subjects to study? Our best answer is: "Learn as much as possible about the class of positions for which you've applied." The exam will test the knowledge, skills and abilities needed to do the work.

Your most valuable source of information about the position you want is the official exam announcement. This announcement lists the training and experience qualifications. Check these standards and apply only if you come reasonably close to meeting them. Many jurisdictions preview the written test in the exam announcement by including a section called "Knowledge and Abilities Required," "Scope of the Examination," or some similar heading. Here you will find out specifically what fields will be tested.

2) Choose appropriate study materials

If the position for which you are applying is technical or advanced, you will read more advanced, specialized material. If you are already familiar with the basic principles of your field, elementary textbooks would waste your time. Concentrate on advanced textbooks and technical periodicals. Think through the concepts and review difficult problems in your field.

These are all general sources. You can get more ideas on your own initiative, following these leads. For example, training manuals and publications of the government agency which employs workers in your field can be useful, particularly for technical and professional positions. A letter or visit to the government department involved may result in more specific study suggestions, and certainly will provide you with a more definite idea of the exact nature of the position you are seeking.

3) Study this book!

III. KINDS OF TESTS

Tests are used for purposes other than measuring knowledge and ability to perform specified duties. For some positions, it is equally important to test ability to make adjustments to new situations or to profit from training. In others, basic mental abilities not dependent on information are essential. Questions which test these things may not appear as pertinent to the duties of the position as those which test for knowledge and information. Yet they are often highly important parts of a fair examination. For very general questions, it is almost impossible to help you direct your study efforts. What we can do is to point out some of the more common of these general abilities needed in public service positions and describe some typical questions.

1) General information

Broad, general information has been found useful for predicting job success in some kinds of work. This is tested in a variety of ways, from vocabulary lists to questions about current events. Basic background in some field of work, such as sociology or economics, may be sampled in a group of questions. Often these are principles which have become familiar to most persons through exposure rather than through formal training. It is difficult to advise you how to study for these questions; being alert to the world around you is our best suggestion.

2) Verbal ability

An example of an ability needed in many positions is verbal or language ability. Verbal ability is, in brief, the ability to use and understand words. Vocabulary and grammar tests are typical measures of this ability. Reading comprehension or paragraph interpretation questions are common in many kinds of civil service tests. You are given a paragraph of written material and asked to find its central meaning.

IV. KINDS OF QUESTIONS

1. Multiple-choice Questions

Most popular of the short-answer questions is the "multiple choice" or "best answer" question. It can be used, for example, to test for factual knowledge, ability to solve problems or judgment in meeting situations found at work.

A multiple-choice question is normally one of three types:

- It can begin with an incomplete statement followed by several possible endings. You are to find the one ending which best completes the statement, although some of the others may not be entirely wrong.
- It can also be a complete statement in the form of a question which is answered by choosing one of the statements listed.
- It can be in the form of a problem – again you select the best answer.

Here is an example of a multiple-choice question with a discussion which should give you some clues as to the method for choosing the right answer:

When an employee has a complaint about his assignment, the action which will best help him overcome his difficulty is to

A. discuss his difficulty with his coworkers
B. take the problem to the head of the organization
C. take the problem to the person who gave him the assignment
D. say nothing to anyone about his complaint

In answering this question, you should study each of the choices to find which is best. Consider choice "A" – Certainly an employee may discuss his complaint with fellow employees, but no change or improvement can result, and the complaint remains unresolved. Choice "B" is a poor choice since the head of the organization probably does not know what assignment you have been given, and taking your problem to him is known as "going over the head" of the supervisor. The supervisor, or person who made the assignment, is the person who can clarify it or correct any injustice. Choice "C" is, therefore, correct. To say nothing, as in choice "D," is unwise. Supervisors have and interest in knowing the problems employees are facing, and the employee is seeking a solution to his problem.

2. True/False

3. Matching Questions

Matching an answer from a column of choices within another column.

V. RECORDING YOUR ANSWERS

Computer terminals are used more and more today for many different kinds of exams.

For an examination with very few applicants, you may be told to record your answers in the test booklet itself. Separate answer sheets are much more common. If this separate answer sheet is to be scored by machine – and this is often the case – it is highly important that you mark your answers correctly in order to get credit.

VI. BEFORE THE TEST

YOUR PHYSICAL CONDITION IS IMPORTANT

If you are not well, you can't do your best work on tests. If you are half asleep, you can't do your best either. Here are some tips:

1) Get about the same amount of sleep you usually get. Don't stay up all night before the test, either partying or worrying—DON'T DO IT!
2) If you wear glasses, be sure to wear them when you go to take the test. This goes for hearing aids, too.
3) If you have any physical problems that may keep you from doing your best, be sure to tell the person giving the test. If you are sick or in poor health, you relay cannot do your best on any test. You can always come back and take the test some other time.

Common sense will help you find procedures to follow to get ready for an examination. Too many of us, however, overlook these sensible measures. Indeed, nervousness and fatigue have been found to be the most serious reasons why applicants fail to do their best on civil service tests. Here is a list of reminders:

- Begin your preparation early – Don't wait until the last minute to go scurrying around for books and materials or to find out what the position is all about.
- Prepare continuously – An hour a night for a week is better than an all-night cram session. This has been definitely established. What is more, a night a week for a month will return better dividends than crowding your study into a shorter period of time.
- Locate the place of the exam – You have been sent a notice telling you when and where to report for the examination. If the location is in a different town or otherwise unfamiliar to you, it would be well to inquire the best route and learn something about the building.
- Relax the night before the test – Allow your mind to rest. Do not study at all that night. Plan some mild recreation or diversion; then go to bed early and get a good night's sleep.
- Get up early enough to make a leisurely trip to the place for the test – This way unforeseen events, traffic snarls, unfamiliar buildings, etc. will not upset you.
- Dress comfortably – A written test is not a fashion show. You will be known by number and not by name, so wear something comfortable.
- Leave excess paraphernalia at home – Shopping bags and odd bundles will get in your way. You need bring only the items mentioned in the official notice you received; usually everything you need is provided. Do not bring reference books to the exam. They will only confuse those last minutes and be taken away from you when in the test room.

- Arrive somewhat ahead of time – If because of transportation schedules you must get there very early, bring a newspaper or magazine to take your mind off yourself while waiting.
- Locate the examination room – When you have found the proper room, you will be directed to the seat or part of the room where you will sit. Sometimes you are given a sheet of instructions to read while you are waiting. Do not fill out any forms until you are told to do so; just read them and be prepared.
- Relax and prepare to listen to the instructions
- If you have any physical problem that may keep you from doing your best, be sure to tell the test administrator. If you are sick or in poor health, you really cannot do your best on the exam. You can come back and take the test some other time.

VII. AT THE TEST

The day of the test is here and you have the test booklet in your hand. The temptation to get going is very strong. Caution! There is more to success than knowing the right answers. You must know how to identify your papers and understand variations in the type of short-answer question used in this particular examination. Follow these suggestions for maximum results from your efforts:

1) Cooperate with the monitor

The test administrator has a duty to create a situation in which you can be as much at ease as possible. He will give instructions, tell you when to begin, check to see that you are marking your answer sheet correctly, and so on. He is not there to guard you, although he will see that your competitors do not take unfair advantage. He wants to help you do your best.

2) Listen to all instructions

Don't jump the gun! Wait until you understand all directions. In most civil service tests you get more time than you need to answer the questions. So don't be in a hurry. Read each word of instructions until you clearly understand the meaning. Study the examples, listen to all announcements and follow directions. Ask questions if you do not understand what to do.

3) Identify your papers

Civil service exams are usually identified by number only. You will be assigned a number; you must not put your name on your test papers. Be sure to copy your number correctly. Since more than one exam may be given, copy your exact examination title.

4) Plan your time

Unless you are told that a test is a "speed" or "rate of work" test, speed itself is usually not important. Time enough to answer all the questions will be provided, but this does not mean that you have all day. An overall time limit has been set. Divide the total time (in minutes) by the number of questions to determine the approximate time you have for each question.

5) Do not linger over difficult questions

If you come across a difficult question, mark it with a paper clip (useful to have along) and come back to it when you have been through the booklet. One caution if you do this – be sure to skip a number on your answer sheet as well. Check often to be sure that you have not lost your place and that you are marking in the row numbered the same as the question you are answering.

6) Read the questions

Be sure you know what the question asks! Many capable people are unsuccessful because they failed to read the questions correctly.

7) Answer all questions

Unless you have been instructed that a penalty will be deducted for incorrect answers, it is better to guess than to omit a question.

8) Speed tests

It is often better NOT to guess on speed tests. It has been found that on timed tests people are tempted to spend the last few seconds before time is called in marking answers at random – without even reading them – in the hope of picking up a few extra points. To discourage this practice, the instructions may warn you that your score will be "corrected" for guessing. That is, a penalty will be applied. The incorrect answers will be deducted from the correct ones, or some other penalty formula will be used.

9) Review your answers

If you finish before time is called, go back to the questions you guessed or omitted to give them further thought. Review other answers if you have time.

10) Return your test materials

If you are ready to leave before others have finished or time is called, take ALL your materials to the monitor and leave quietly. Never take any test material with you. The monitor can discover whose papers are not complete, and taking a test booklet may be grounds for disqualification.

VIII. EXAMINATION TECHNIQUES

1) Read the general instructions carefully. These are usually printed on the first page of the exam booklet. As a rule, these instructions refer to the timing of the examination; the fact that you should not start work until the signal and must stop work at a signal, etc. If there are any special instructions, such as a choice of questions to be answered, make sure that you note this instruction carefully.

2) When you are ready to start work on the examination, that is as soon as the signal has been given, read the instructions to each question booklet, underline any key words or phrases, such as least, best, outline, describe and the like. In this way you will tend to answer as requested rather than discover on reviewing your paper that you listed without describing, that you selected the worst choice rather than the best choice, etc.

3) If the examination is of the objective or multiple-choice type – that is, each question will also give a series of possible answers: A, B, C or D, and you are called upon to select the best answer and write the letter next to that answer on your answer paper – it is advisable to start answering each question in turn. There may be anywhere from 50 to 100 such questions in the three or four hours allotted and you can see how much time would be taken if you read through all the questions before beginning to answer any. Furthermore, if you

come across a question or group of questions which you know would be difficult to answer, it would undoubtedly affect your handling of all the other questions.

4) If the examination is of the essay type and contains but a few questions, it is a moot point as to whether you should read all the questions before starting to answer any one. Of course, if you are given a choice – say five out of seven and the like – then it is essential to read all the questions so you can eliminate the two that are most difficult. If, however, you are asked to answer all the questions, there may be danger in trying to answer the easiest one first because you may find that you will spend too much time on it. The best technique is to answer the first question, then proceed to the second, etc.

5) Time your answers. Before the exam begins, write down the time it started, then add the time allowed for the examination and write down the time it must be completed, then divide the time available somewhat as follows:
   - If 3-1/2 hours are allowed, that would be 210 minutes. If you have 80 objective-type questions, that would be an average of 2-1/2 minutes per question. Allow yourself no more than 2 minutes per question, or a total of 160 minutes, which will permit about 50 minutes to review.
   - If for the time allotment of 210 minutes there are 7 essay questions to answer, that would average about 30 minutes a question. Give yourself only 25 minutes per question so that you have about 35 minutes to review.

6) The most important instruction is to read each question and make sure you know what is wanted. The second most important instruction is to time yourself properly so that you answer every question. The third most important instruction is to answer every question. Guess if you have to but include something for each question. Remember that you will receive no credit for a blank and will probably receive some credit if you write something in answer to an essay question. If you guess a letter – say "B" for a multiple-choice question – you may have guessed right. If you leave a blank as an answer to a multiple-choice question, the examiners may respect your feelings but it will not add a point to your score. Some exams may penalize you for wrong answers, so in such cases only, you may not want to guess unless you have some basis for your answer.

7) Suggestions
   a. Objective-type questions
      1. Examine the question booklet for proper sequence of pages and questions
      2. Read all instructions carefully
      3. Skip any question which seems too difficult; return to it after all other questions have been answered
      4. Apportion your time properly; do not spend too much time on any single question or group of questions
      5. Note and underline key words – all, most, fewest, least, best, worst, same, opposite, etc.
      6. Pay particular attention to negatives
      7. Note unusual option, e.g., unduly long, short, complex, different or similar in content to the body of the question
      8. Observe the use of "hedging" words – probably, may, most likely, etc.

9. Make sure that your answer is put next to the same number as the question
10. Do not second-guess unless you have good reason to believe the second answer is definitely more correct
11. Cross out original answer if you decide another answer is more accurate; do not erase until you are ready to hand your paper in
12. Answer all questions; guess unless instructed otherwise
13. Leave time for review

b. Essay questions
1. Read each question carefully
2. Determine exactly what is wanted. Underline key words or phrases.
3. Decide on outline or paragraph answer
4. Include many different points and elements unless asked to develop any one or two points or elements
5. Show impartiality by giving pros and cons unless directed to select one side only
6. Make and write down any assumptions you find necessary to answer the questions
7. Watch your English, grammar, punctuation and choice of words
8. Time your answers; don't crowd material

8) Answering the essay question

Most essay questions can be answered by framing the specific response around several key words or ideas. Here are a few such key words or ideas:

M's: manpower, materials, methods, money, management
P's: purpose, program, policy, plan, procedure, practice, problems, pitfalls, personnel, public relations

a. Six basic steps in handling problems:
1. Preliminary plan and background development
2. Collect information, data and facts
3. Analyze and interpret information, data and facts
4. Analyze and develop solutions as well as make recommendations
5. Prepare report and sell recommendations
6. Install recommendations and follow up effectiveness

b. Pitfalls to avoid
1. Taking things for granted – A statement of the situation does not necessarily imply that each of the elements is necessarily true; for example, a complaint may be invalid and biased so that all that can be taken for granted is that a complaint has been registered
2. Considering only one side of a situation – Wherever possible, indicate several alternatives and then point out the reasons you selected the best one
3. Failing to indicate follow up – Whenever your answer indicates action on your part, make certain that you will take proper follow-up action to see how successful your recommendations, procedures or actions turn out to be
4. Taking too long in answering any single question – Remember to time your answers properly

EXAMINATION SECTION

EXAMINATION SECTION

TEST 1

DIRECTIONS: Each question or incomplete statement is followed by several suggested answers or completions. Select the one that BEST answers the question or completes the statement. *PRINT THE LETTER OF THE CORRECT ANSWER IN THE SPACE AT THE RIGHT.*

1. At times there may be a conflict between employees' needs and agency goals. A supervisor's MAIN role in motivating employees in such circumstances is to try to 1.____
   A. develop good work habits among the employees whom he supervises
   B. emphasize the importance of material rewards such as merit increases
   C. keep careful records of employees' performance for possible disciplinary action
   D. reconcile employees' objectives with those of the public agency

2. Organizations cannot function effectively without policies. However, when an organization imposes excessively detailed policy restrictions, it is MOST likely to lead to 2.____
   A. conflicts among individual employees
   B. a lack of adequate supervision
   C. a reduction of employee initiative
   D. a reliance on punitive discipline

3. The PRIMARY responsibility for establishing good employee relations in the public service usually rests with 3.____
   A. employees
   B. management
   C. civil service organizations
   D. employee organizations

4. At times, certain off-the-job conduct of public employees may be of concern to management. This concern stems from the fact that 4.____
   A. agency programs could be harmed by adverse publicity if employees' conduct is considered detrimental by the public
   B. fairness to all concerned is usually the major consideration in disciplinary cases
   C. public employees must meet higher standards than employees working in private industry
   D. public employees have high ethical standards and may participate in social action programs

5. At one time or another, most employees ask for, or expect, special treatment. For a supervisor faced with this problem, the one of the following which is the MOST valid guideline is: 5.____
   A. According to the rules, a supervisor must give identical treatment to all his subordinates, regardless of the circumstances.

B. Although all employees have equal rights, it is sometimes necessary to give an employee special treatment to meet an individual need.
C. It would damage morale if any employee were to receive special treatment, regardless of circumstances.
D. Since each employee has different needs, there is little reason to maintain general rules.

6. Mental health problems exist in many parts of our society and may also be found in the work setting. 6.____
The BASIC role of the supervisor in relation to the mental health problems of his subordinates is to
A. restrict himself solely to the taking of disciplinary measures, if warranted, and follow up carefully
B. avoid involvement in personal matters
C. identify mental health problems as early as possible
D. resolve mental health problems through personal counseling

7. Supervisory expectation of high levels of employee performance, where such performance is possible, is MOST likely to lead to employees' 7.____
A. expecting frequent praise and encouragement
B. gaining a greater sense of satisfaction
C. needing less detailed instructions than previously
D. reducing their quantitative output

8. In public agencies, as elsewhere, supervisors sometimes compete with one another to increase their units' productivity. 8.____
Of the following, the MAJOR disadvantage of such competition, from the general viewpoint of providing good public service, is that
A. while individual employee effort will increase, unit productivity will decrease
B. employees will be discouraged from sincere interest in their work
C. the supervisors' competition may hinder the achievement of agency goals
D. total payroll costs will increase as the activities of each unit increase

9. If employees are motivated primarily by material compensation, the amount of effort an individual employee will put into performing his work effectively will depend MAINLY upon how he perceives 9.____
A. cooperation to be tied to successful effort
B. the association between good work and increased compensation
C. the public status of his particular position
D. the supervisor's behavior in work situations

10. Cash awards to individual employees are sometimes used to encourage useful suggestions. However, some management experts believe that awards should involve some form of employee recognition other than cash. 10.____
Which of the following reasons BEST supports opposition to using cash as a reward for worthwhile suggestions?

A. Cash awards cause employees to expend excessive time in making suggestions.
B. Taxpayer opposition to dash awards has increased following generous salary increases for public employees in recent years.
C. Public funds expended on awards leads to a poor image of public employees.
D. The use of cash awards raises the problem of deciding the monetary value of suggestions.

11. The BEST general rule for a supervisor to follow in giving praise and criticism is to 11.____
A. criticize and praise publicly
B. criticize publicly and praise privately
C. praise and criticize privately
D. praise publicly and criticize privately

12. An important step in designing an error-control policy is to determine the maximum number of errors that can be considered acceptable for the entire organization. 12.____
Of the following, the MOST important factor in making such a decision is the
A. number of clerical staff available to check for errors
B. frequency of errors by supervisors
C. human and material costs of errors
D. number of errors that will become known to the public

13. When a supervisor tries to correct a situation where errors have been widespread, he should concentrate his efforts, and those of the employees involved, on 13.____
A. avoiding future mistakes
B. fixing appropriate blame
C. preparing a written report
D. determining fair penalties

14. When delegating work to a subordinate, a supervisor should ALWAYS tell the subordinate 14.____
A. each step in the procedure for doing the work
B. how much time to expend
C. what is to be accomplished
D. whether reports are necessary

15. The responsibilities of all employees should be clearly defined and understood. In addition, in order for employees to successfully fulfill their responsibilities, they should also GENERALLY be given 15.____
A. written directives
B. close supervision
C. corresponding authority
D. daily instructions

16. The one of the following types of training in which positive transfer of training to the actual work situation is MOST likely to take place is _____ training. 16.____
A. conference
B. demonstration
C. classroom
D. on-the-job

17. The type of training or instruction in which the subject matter is presented in small units called frames is known as 17.____
   A. programmed instruction
   B. reinforcement
   C. remediation
   D. skills training

18. In order to bring about maximum learning in a training situation, a supervisor acting as a trainer should attempt to create a setting in which 18.____
   A. all trainees experience a large amount of failure as an incentive
   B. all trainees experience a small amount of failure as an incentive
   C. each trainee experiences approximately the same amounts of success and failure
   D. each trainee experiences as much success and as little failure as possible

19. Assume that, in a training course given by an agency, the instructor conducts a brief quiz, on paper, toward the close of each session. 19.____
From the point of view of maximizing learning, it would be BEST for the instructor to
   A. wait until the last session to provide the correct answers
   B. give the correct answers aloud immediately after each quiz
   C. permit trainees to take the questions home with them so that they can look up the answers
   D. wait until the next session to provide the correct answers

20. A supervisor, in the course of evaluating employees, should ALWAYS determine whether 20.____
   A. employees realize that their work is under scrutiny
   B. the ratings will be included in permanent records
   C. employees meet standards of performance
   D. his statements on the rating form are similar to those made by the previous supervisor

21. All of the following are legitimate objectives of employee performance reporting systems EXCEPT 21.____
   A. serving as a check on personnel policies such as job qualification requirements and placement techniques
   B. determining who is the least efficient worker among a large number of employees
   C. improving employee performance by identifying strong and weak points in individual performance
   D. developing standards of satisfactory performance

22. Studies of existing employee performance evaluation schemes have revealed a common tendency to construct guides in order to measure <u>inferred</u> traits. 22.____
Of the following, the BEST example of an inferred trait is
   A. appearance
   B. loyalty
   C. accuracy
   D. promptness

23. Which of the following is MOST likely to be a positive influence in promoting common agreement at a staff conference? 23.____
    A. A mature, tolerant group of participants
    B. A strong chairman with firm opinions
    C. The normal differences of human personalities
    D. The urge to forcefully support one's views

24. Before holding a problem-solving conference, the conference leader sent to each invitee an announcement on which he listed the names of all invitees. 24.____
    His action in listing the names was
    A. *wise*, mainly because all invitees will know who has been invited, and can, if necessary, plan a proper approach
    B. *unwise*, mainly because certain invitees could form factions prior to the conference
    C. *unwise*, mainly because invitees might come to the conference in a belligerent mood if they had had interpersonal conflicts with other invitees
    D. *wise*, mainly because invitees who are antagonistic to each other could decide not to attend

25. Methods analysis is a detailed study of existing or proposed work methods for the purpose of improving agency operations. 25.____
    Of the following, it is MOST accurate to say that this type of study
    A. can sometimes be made informally by the experienced supervisor who can identify problems and suggest solutions
    B. is not suitable for studying the operations of a public agency
    C. will be successfully accomplished only if an outside organization reviews agency operations
    D. usually costs more to complete than is justified by the potential economies to be realized

KEY (CORRECT ANSWERS)

1.	D	11.	D
2.	C	12.	C
3.	B	13.	A
4.	A	14.	C
5.	B	15.	C
6.	C	16.	D
7.	B	17.	A
8.	C	18.	D
9.	B	19.	B
10.	D	20.	C

21.
22. B
23. A
24. A
25. A

TEST 2

DIRECTIONS: Each question or incomplete statement is followed by several suggested answers or completions. Select the one that BEST answers the question or completes the statement. *PRINT THE LETTER OF THE CORRECT ANSWER IN THE SPACE AT THE RIGHT.*

1. Present-day managerial practices advocate that adequate hierarchical levels of communication be maintained among all levels of management. 1.____
Of the following, the BEST way to accomplish this is with
   A. intradepartmental memoranda only
   B. interdepartmental memoranda only
   C. periodic staff meetings, interdepartmental and intradepartmental memoranda
   D. interdepartmental and intradepartmental memoranda

2. It is generally agreed upon that it is important to have effective communications in the unit so that everyone knows exactly what is expected of him. 2.____
Of the following, the communications system which can assist in fulfilling this objective BEST is one which consists of
   A. written policies and procedures for administrative functions and verbal policies and procedures for professional functions
   B. written policies and procedures for professional and administrative functions
   C. verbal policies and procedures for professional and administrative functions
   D. verbal policies and procedures for professional functions

3. If a department manager wishes to build an effective department, he MOST generally must 3.____
   A. be able to hire and fire as he feels necessary
   B. consider the total aspects of his job, his influence and the effects of his decisions
   C. have access to reasonable amounts of personnel and money with which to build his programs
   D. attend as many professional conferences as possible so that he can keep up-to-date with all the latest advances in the field

4. Of the following, the factor which generally contributes MOST effectively to the performance of the unit is that the supervisor 4.____
   A. personally inspect the work of all employees
   B. fill orders at a faster rate than his subordinates
   C. have an exact knowledge of theory
   D. implement a program of professional development for his staff

5. Administrative policies relate MOST closely to 5.____
   A. control of commodities and personnel
   B. general policies emanating from the central office
   C. fiscal management of the department only
   D. handling and dispensing of funds

6. Part of being a good supervisor is to be able to develop an attitude towards employees which will motivate them to do their best on the job. 6.____
The GOOD supervisor, therefore, should
   A. take an interest in subordinates, but not develop an all-consuming attitude in this area
   B. remain in an aloof position when dealing with employees
   C. be as close to subordinates as possible on the job
   D. take a complete interest in all the activities of subordinates, both on and off the job

7. The practice of a supervisor assigning an experienced employee to train new employees instead of training them himself is GENERALLY considered 7.____
   A. *undesirable*; the more experienced employee will resent being taken away from his regular job
   B. *desirable*; the supervisor can then devote more time to his regular duties
   C. *undesirable*; the more experienced employee is not working at the proper level to train new employees
   D. *desirable*; the more experienced employee is probably a better trainer than the supervisor

8. It is generally agreed that on-the-job training is MOST effective when new employees are 8.____
   A. provided with study manuals, standard operating procedures and other written materials to be studied for at least two weeks before the employees attempt to do the job
   B. shown how to do the job in detail, and then instructed to do the work under close supervision
   C. trained by an experienced worker for at least a week to make certain that the employees can do the job
   D. given work immediately which is checked at the end of each day

9. Employees sometimes form small informal groups, commonly called cliques. With regard to the effect of such groups on processing of the workload, the attitude a supervisor should take towards these cliques is that of 9.____
   A. *acceptance*, since they take the employees' minds off their work without wasting too much time
   B. *rejection*, since those workers inside the clique tend to do less work than the outsiders
   C. *acceptance*, since the supervisor is usually included in the clique
   D. *rejection*, since they are usually disliked by higher management

10. Of the following, the BEST statement regarding rules and regulations in a unit is that they 10.____
   A. are "necessary evils" to be tolerated by those at and above the first supervisory level only
   B. are stated in broad, indefinite terms so as to allow maximum amount of leeway in complying with them

C. must be understood by all employees in the unit
D. are primarily for management's needs since insurance regulations mandate them

11. It is sometimes considered desirable for a supervisor to survey the opinions of his employees before taking action on decisions affecting them. 11.____
Of the following the greatest DISADVANTAGE of following this approach is that the employees might
A. use this opportunity to complain rather than to make constructive suggestions
B. lose respect for their supervisor whom they feel cannot make his own decisions
C. regard this as an attempt by the supervisor to get ideas for which he can later claim credit
D. be resentful if their suggestions are not adopted

12. Of the following, the MOST important reason for keeping statements of duties of employees up-to-date is to 12.____
A. serve as a basis of information for other governmental jurisdictions
B. enable the department of personnel to develop job-related examinations
C. differentiate between levels within the occupational groups
D. enable each employee to know what his duties are

13. Of the following, the BEST way to evaluate the progress of a new subordinate is to 13.____
A. compare the output of the new employee from week to week as to quantity and quality
B. obtain the opinions of the new employee's co-workers
C. test the new employee periodically to see how much he has learned
D. hold frequent discussions with the employee focusing on his work

14. Of the following, a supervisor is LEAST likely to contribute to good morale in the unit if he 14.____
A. encourages employees to increase their knowledge and proficiency in their work on their own time
B. reprimands subordinates uniformly when infractions are committed
C. refuses to accept explanations for mistakes regardless of who has made them or how serious they are
D. compliments subordinates for superior work performance in the presence of their peers

15. The practice of promoting supervisors from within a given unit only, rather than from within the entire agency, may BEST be described as 15.____
A. *desirable*, because the type of work in each unit generally is substantially different from all other units
B. *undesirable*, since it will severely reduce the number of eligible from which to select a supervisor

C. *desirable*, since it enables each employee to know in advance the precise extent of promotion opportunities in his unit
D. *undesirable*, because it creates numerous administrative and budgetary difficulties

16. Of the following, the BEST way for a supervisor to make assignments GENERALLY is to 16.____
A. give the easier assignments to employees with greater seniority
B. give the difficult assignments to the employees with greater seniority
C. make assignments according to the ability of each employee
D. rotate the assignments among the employees

17. Assume that a supervisor makes a proposal through appropriate channels which would delegate final authority and responsibility to a subordinate employee for a major control function within the agency. 17.____
According to current management theory, this proposal should be
A. *adopted*, since this would enable the supervisor to devote more time to non-routine tasks
B. *rejected*, since final responsibility for this high-level assignment may not properly be delegated to a subordinate employee
C. *adopted*, since the assignment of increased responsibility to subordinate employees is a vital part of their development and training
D. *rejected*, since the morale of the subordinate employees not selected for this assignment would be adversely affected

18. If it becomes necessary for a supervisor to improve the performance of a subordinate to assure the achievement of results according to plans, the BEST course of action, of the following, generally would be to 18.____
A. emphasize the subordinate's strengths and try to motivate the employee to improve on those factors
B. emphasize the subordinate's weak areas of performance and try to bring them up to an acceptable standard
C. issue a memorandum to all employees warning that if performance does not improve, disciplinary measures will be taken
D. transfer the subordinate to another section engaged in different work

19. A supervisor who specifies each phase of a job in detail supervises closely and permits very little discretion in performance of tasks GENERALLY 19.____
A. provides motivation for his staff to produce more work
B. finds that his subordinate make fewer mistakes than those with minimal supervision
C. finds that his subordinates have little or no incentive to work any harder than necessary
D. provides superior training opportunities for his employees

20. Assume that you supervise two employees who do not get along well with each other. Their relationship has been continuously deteriorating. You decide to take steps to solve this problem by first determining the reason for their inability to get along with each other. 20.____
This course of action is
   A. *desirable*, because their work is probably adversely affected by their differences
   B. *undesirable*, because your inquiries might be misinterpreted by the employees and cause resentment
   C. *desirable*, because you could then learn who is at fault for causing the deteriorating relationship and take appropriate disciplinary measures
   D. *undesirable*, because it is best to let them work their differences out between themselves

21. Routine procedures that have worked well in the past should be reviewed periodically by a supervisor MAINLY because 21.____
   A. they may have become outdated or in need of revision
   B. employees may dislike the procedures even though they have proven successful in the past
   C. these reviews are the main part of a supervisor's job
   D. this practice serves to give the supervisor an idea of how productive his subordinates are

22. Assume that an employee tells his supervisor about a grievance he has against a co-worker. The supervisor assures the employee that he will immediately take action to eliminate the grievance. 22.____
The supervisor's attitude should be considered
   A. *correct*, because a good supervisor is one who can come to a quick decision
   B. *incorrect*, because the supervisor should have told the employee that he will investigate the grievance and then determine a future course of action
   C. *correct*, because the employee's morale will be higher, resulting in greater productivity
   D. *incorrect*, because the supervisor should remain uninvolved and let the employees settle grievances between themselves

23. If an employee's work output is low and of poor quality due to faulty work habits, the MOST constructive of the following ways for a supervisor to correct this situation *generally* is to 23.____
   A. discipline the employee
   B. transfer the employee to another unit
   C. provide additional training
   D. check the employee's work continuously

24. Assume that it becomes necessary for a supervisor to ask his staff to work overtime. 24.____
Which one of the following techniques is MOST likely to win their willing cooperation to do this?

A. Point out that this is part of their job specification entitled “performs related work”
B. Explain the reason it is necessary for the employees to work overtime
C. Promise the employees special consideration regarding future leave matters
D. Warn that if the employees do not work overtime, they will face possible disciplinary action

25. If an employee’s work performance has recently fallen below established minimum standards for quality and quantity, the threat of demotion or other disciplinary measures as an attempt to improve this employee’s performance would probably be the MOST acceptable and effective course of action 25.____
A. *only* after other more constructive measures have failed
B. *if* applied uniformly to all employees as soon as performance falls below standard
C. *only* if the employee understands that the threat will not actually be carried out
D. *if* the employee is promised that, as soon as his work performance improves, he will be reinstated to his previous status

---

KEY (CORRECT ANSWERS)

1.	C	11.	D
2.	B	12.	D
3.	B	13.	A
4.	D	14.	C
5.	A	15.	B
6.	A	16.	C
7.	B	17.	B
8.	B	18.	B
9.	A	19.	C
10.	C	20.	A

21.	A
22.	B
23.	C
24.	B
25.	A

TEST 3

DIRECTIONS: Each question or incomplete statement is followed by several suggested answers or completions. Select the one that BEST answers the question or completes the statement. *PRINT THE LETTER OF THE CORRECT ANSWER IN THE SPACE AT THE RIGHT.*

1. If, as a supervisor, it becomes necessary for you to assign an employee to supervise your unit during your vacation, it would generally be BEST to select the employee who 1.____
   A. is the best technician on the staff
   B. can get the work out smoothly, without friction
   C. has the most seniority
   D. is the most popular with the group

2. Assume that, as a supervisor, your own work has accumulated to the point where you decide that it is desirable for you to delegate in order to meet your deadlines. 2.____
   The one of the following tasks which would be MOST appropriate to delegate to a subordinate is
   A. checking the work of the employees for accuracy
   B. attending a staff conference at which implementation of a new departmental policy will be discussed
   C. preparing a final report including a recommendation on purchase of expensive new laboratory equipment
   D. preparing final budget estimates for next year's budget

3. Of the following actions, the one LEAST appropriate for you to take during an initial interview with a new employee is to 3.____
   A. find out about the experience and education of the new employee
   B. attempt to determine for what job in your unit the employee would best be suited
   C. tell the employee about his duties and responsibilities
   D. ascertain whether the employee will make good promotion material

4. If it becomes necessary to reprimand a subordinate employee, the BEST of the following ways to do this is to 4.____
   A. ask the employee to stay after working hours and then reprimand him
   B. reprimand the employee immediately after the infraction has been committed
   C. take the employee aside and speak to him privately during regular working hours
   D. write a short memo to the employee warning that strict adherence to departmental policy and procedures is required of all employees

5. If you, as a supervisor, believe that one of your subordinate employees has a serious problem, such as alcoholism or an emotional disturbance, which is adversely affecting his work, the BEST way to handle this situation *initially* would be to 5.____

A. urge him to seek proper professional help before he is dismissed from his job
B. ignore it and let the employee work out the problem himself
C. suggest that the employee take an extended leave of absence until he can again function effectively
D. frankly tell the employee that unless his work improves, you will take disciplinary measures against him

6. Of the following, the BEST way to develop a subordinate's potential is to 6.____
A. give him a fair chance to learn by doing
B. assign him more than his share of work
C. criticize only his work
D. urge him to do his work rapidly

7. During a survey, an employee from another agency asks you to assist him on a job which would require a full day of your time. 7.____
Of the following, the BEST immediate action for you to take is to
A. refuse to assist him
B. ask for compensation before doing it
C. assist him promptly
D. notify his department head

8. Of the following, the BEST way to handle an overly talkative subordinate is to 8.____
A. have your superior talk to him about it
B. have a subordinate talk to him about it
C. talk to him about it in a group conference
D. talk to him about it in private

9. While you are making a survey, a citizen questions you about the work you are doing. 9.____
Of the following, the BEST thing to do is to
A. answer the questions tactfully
B. refuse to answer any questions
C. advise him to write a letter to the main office
D. answer the questions in double-talk

10. Respect for a supervisor is MOST likely to increase if he is 10.____
A. morose
B. sporadic
C. vindictive
D. zealous

11. A subordinate who continuously bypasses his immediate supervisor for technical information should be 11.____
A. reprimanded by his immediate supervisor
B. ignored by his immediate supervisor
C. given more difficult work to do
D. given less difficult work to do

12. Complicated instructions should NOT be written 12.____
A. accurately
B. lucidly
C. factually
D. verbosely

13. Of the following, the MOST important reason for checking a report is to 13.____
    A. check accuracy
    B. eliminate unnecessary sections
    C. catch mistakes
    D. check for delineation

14. Two subordinates under your supervision dislike each other to the extent that production is cut down. 14.____
    Your BEST action as a supervisor is to
    A. ignore the matter and hope for the best
    B. transfer the more aggressive man
    C. cut down on the workload
    D. talk to them together about the matter

15. One of the following characteristics which a supervisor should NOT display while explaining a job to a subordinate is 15.____
    A. enthusiasm
    B. confidence
    C. apathy
    D. determination

16. Of the following, for BEST production of work, it should be assigned according to a person's 16.____
    A. attitude toward the work
    B. ability to do the work
    C. salary
    D. seniority

17. You receive an anonymous written complaint from a citizen about a subordinate who used abusive language. 17.____
    Of the following, your BEST course of action is to
    A. ignore the letter
    B. report it to your supervisor
    C. discuss the complaint with the subordinate privately
    D. keep the subordinate in the office

18. A supervisor should recognize that the way to get the BEST results from his instructions and assignments to the staff is to use 18.____
    A. a suggestive approach after he has decided exactly what is to be done and how
    B. the willing and cooperative staff members and avoid the hard-to-handle people
    C. care to select the persons most capable of carrying out the assignments
    D. an authoritative, non-nonsense tone when issuing instructions or giving assignments

19. As the supervisor of a unit, you find that you are spending too much of your time on routine tasks and not enough on coordinating the work of the staff or preparing necessary reports. 19.____
    Of the following, it would be MOST advisable for you to
    A. discard a great portion of the routine jobs done in the unit
    B. give some of the routine jobs to other members of the staff
    C. postpone the routine jobs and concentrate on coordinating the work of the staff
    D. delegate the job of coordinating the work to the most capable member of the staff

20. At times a supervisor may be called upon to train new employees. Suppose that you are giving such training in several sessions to be held on different days. During the first session, a trainee interrupts several times to ask questions at key points in your discussion. 20.____
Of the following, the BEST way to handle this trainee is to
   A. advise him to pay closer attention so he can avoid asking too many questions
   B. tell him to listen without interrupting and he'll hear his questions answered
   C. answer his questions to show him that you know your field, but make a mental note that this trainee is a troublemaker
   D. answer each question fully and make certain he understands the answers

21. Employee errors can be reduced to a minimum by effective supervision and by training. 21.____
Which of the following approaches used by a supervisor would usually be MOST effective in handling an employee who has made an avoidable and serious error for the first time?
   A. Tell the worker how other employees avoid making errors
   B. Analyze with the employee the situation leading to the error and then take whatever administrative or training steps are needed to avoid such errors
   C. Use this error as the basis for a staff meeting at which the employee's error is disclosed and discussed in an effort to improve the performance
   D. Urge the employee to modify his behavior in light of his mistake

22. Suppose that a particular staff member, formerly one of your most regular workers, has recently fallen into the habit of arriving a bit late to work several times a week. You feel that such a habit can grow consistently worse and spread to other staff members unless it is checked. 22.____
Of the following, the BEST action for you to take, as the supervisor in charge of the unit, is to
   A. go immediately to your own supervisor, present the facts, and have this employee disciplined
   B. speak privately to this tardy employee, advise him of the need to improve his punctuality, and inform him that he'll be disciplined if late again
   C. talk to the co-worker with whom this late employee is most friendly, and ask the friend to help him solve his tardiness problem
   D. speak privately with this employee, and try to discover and deal with the reasons for the latenesses

23. A supervisor may make an assignment in the form of a request, a command, or a call for volunteers. 23.____
It is LEAST desirable to make an assignment in the form of a request when
   A. an employee does not like the particular kind of assignment to be given
   B. the assignment requires working past the regular closing day
   C. an emergency has come up
   D. the assignment is not particularly pleasant for anybody

24. When you give a certain task that you normally perform yourself to one of your employees, it is MOST important that you 24.____
    A. lead the employee to believe that he has been chosen above others to perform this job
    B. describe the job as important even though it is merely a routine task
    C. explain the job that needs to be accomplished, but always let the employee decide how to do it
    D. tell the employee why you are delegating the job to him and explain exactly what he is to do

25. A supervisor when instructing new trainees in the routine of his unit should include a description of the department's overall objectives and programs in order to 25.____
    A. insure that individual work assignments will be completed satisfactorily
    B. create a favorable impression of his supervisory capabilities
    C. develop a better understanding of the purposes behind work assignments
    D. produce an immediate feeling of group cooperation

KEY (CORRECT ANSWERS)

1. B
2. A
3. D
4. C
5. A

6. A
7. A
8. D
9. A
10. D

11. A
12. D
13. C
14. D
15. C

16. B
17. C
18. C
19. B
20. D

21. B
22. D
23. A
24. D
25. C

TEST 4

DIRECTIONS: Each question or incomplete statement is followed by several suggested answers or completions. Select the one that BEST answers the question or completes the statement. *PRINT THE LETTER OF THE CORRECT ANSWER IN THE SPACE AT THE RIGHT.*

1. An integral part of every supervisor's job is getting his ideas or instructions across to his staff. 1.____
   The extent of his success, if he has a reasonably competent staff, is PRIMARILY dependent on the
   A. interest of the employee
   B. intelligence of the employee
   C. reasoning behind the ideas or instructions
   D. presentation of the ideas or instructions

2. Generally, what is the FIRST action the supervisor should take when an employee approaches him with a complaint? 2.____
   A. Review the employee's recent performance with him
   B. Use the complaint as a basis to discuss improvement of procedures
   C. Find out from the employee the details of the complaint
   D. Advise the employee to take his complaint to the head of the department

3. Of the following, which is NOT usually considered one of the purposes of counseling an employee after an evaluation of his performance? 3.____
   A. Explaining the performance standards used by the supervisor
   B. Discussing necessary discipline action to be taken
   C. Emphasizing the employee's strengths and weaknesses
   D. Planning better utilization of the employee's strengths

4. Assume that a supervisor, when reviewing a decision reached by one of his subordinates, finds the decision incorrect. 4.____
   Under these circumstances, it would be MOST desirable for the supervisor to
   A. correct the decision and inform the subordinate of this at a staff meeting
   B. correct the decision and suggest a more detailed analysis in the future
   C. help the employee find the reason for the correct decision
   D. refrain from assigning this type of a problem to the employee

5. An IMPORTANT characteristic of a good supervisor is his ability to 5.____
   A. be a stern disciplinarian
   B. put off the settling of grievances
   C. solve problems
   D. find fault in individuals

6. A new supervisor will BEST obtain the respect of the men assigned to him if he 6.____
   A. makes decisions rapidly and sticks to the, regardless of whether they are right or wrong
   B. makes decisions rapidly and then changes them just as rapidly if the decisions are wrong
   C. does not make any decisions unless he is absolutely sure that they are right
   D. makes his decisions after considering carefully all available information

7. A newly appointed worker is operating at a level of performance below that of the other employees. 7.____
In this situation, a supervisor should FIRST
   A. lower the acceptable standard for the new man
   B. find out why the new man cannot do as well as the others
   C. advise the new worker he will be dropped from the payroll at the end of the probationary period
   D. assign another new worker to assist the first man

8. Assume that you have to instruct a new man on a specific departmental operation. The new man seems unsure of what you have said. 8.____
Of the following, the BEST way for you to determine whether the man has understood you is to
   A. have the man explain the operation to you in his own words
   B. repeat your explanation to him slowly
   C. repeat your explanation to him, using simpler wording
   D. emphasize the important parts of the operation to him

9. A supervisor realizes that he has taken an instantaneous dislike to a new worker assigned to him. 9.____
The BEST course of action for the supervisor to take in this case is to
   A. be especially observant of the new worker's actions
   B. request that the new worker be reassigned
   C. make a special effort to be fair to the new worker
   D. ask to be transferred himself

10. A supervisor gives detailed instructions to his men as to how a certain type of job is to be done. 10.____
One ADVANTAGE of this practice is that this will
   A. result in a more flexible operation
   B. standardize operations
   C. encourage new men to learn
   D. encourage initiative to learn

11. Of the following the one that would MOST likely be the result of poor planning is: 11.____
   A. Omissions are discovered after the work is completed
   B. During the course of normal inspection, a meter is found to be inaccessible
   C. An inspector completes his assignments for that day ahead of schedule
   D. A problem arises during an inspection and prevents an inspector from completing his day's assignments

12. Of the following, the BEST way for a supervisor to maintain good employee morale is for the supervisor to 12.____
   A. avoid correcting the employee when he makes mistakes
   B. continually praise the employee's work even when it is of average quality
   C. show that he is willing to assist in solving the employee's problems
   D. accept the employee's excuses for failure even though the excuses are not valid

13. A supervisor takes time to explain to his men why a departmental order has been issued. 13.____
This practice is
   A. *good*, mainly because without this explanation the men will not be able to carry out the order
   B. *bad*, mainly because time will be wasted for no useful purpose
   C. *good*, because understanding the reasons behind an order will lead to more effective carrying out of the order
   D. *bad*, because men will then question every order that they receive

14. Of the following, the MOST important responsibility of a supervisor in charge of a section is to 14.____
   A. establish close personal relationships with each of his subordinates in the section
   B. insure that each subordinate in the section knows the full range of his duties and responsibilities
   C. maintain friendly relations with his immediate supervisor
   D. protect his subordinate from criticism from any source

15. The BEST way to get a good work output from employees is to 15.____
   A. hold over them the threat of disciplinary action or removal
   B. maintain a steady, unrelenting pressure on them
   C. show them that you can do anything they can do faster and better
   D. win their respect and liking, so they want to work for you

KEY (CORRECT ANSWERS)

1.	A	6.	D	11.	A
2.	C	7.	B	12.	C
3.	A	8.	A	13.	C
4.	C	9.	C	14.	B
5.	C	10.	B	15.	D

EXAMINATION SECTION

TEST 1

DIRECTIONS: Each question or incomplete statement is followed by several suggested answers or completions. Select the one that BEST answers the question or completes the statement. *PRINT THE LETTER OF THE CORRECT ANSWER IN THE SPACE AT THE RIGHT.*

1. Which of the following is the MOST likely action a supervisor should take to help establish an effective working relationship with his departmental superiors? 1.____
   A. Delay the implementation of new procedures received from superiors in order to evaluate their appropriateness.
   B. Skip the chain of command whenever he feels that it is to his advantage
   C. Keep supervisors informed of problems in his area and the steps taken to correct them
   D. Don't take up superiors' time by discussing anticipated problems but wait until the difficulties occur

2. Of the following, the action a supervisor could take which would generally be MOST conducive to the establishment of an effective working relationship with employees includes 2.____
   A. maintaining impersonal relationships to prevent development of biased actions
   B. treating all employees equally without adjusting for individual differences
   C. continuous observation of employees on the job with insistence on constant improvement
   D. careful planning and scheduling of work for your employees

3. Which of the following procedures is the LEAST likely to establish effective working relationships between employees and supervisors? 3.____
   A. Encouraging two-way communication with employees
   B. Periodic discussion with employees regarding their job performance
   C. Ignoring employees' gripes concerning job difficulties
   D. Avoiding personal prejudices in dealing with employees

4. Criticism can be used as a tool to point out the weak areas of a subordinate's work performance. 4.____
   Of the following, the BEST action for a supervisor to take so that his criticism will be accepted is to
   A. focus his criticism on the act instead of on the person
   B. exaggerate the errors in order to motivate the employee to do better
   C. pass judgment quickly and privately without investigating the circumstances of the error
   D. generalize the criticism and not specifically point out the errors in performance

5. In trying to improve the motivation of his subordinates, a supervisor can achieve the BEST results by taking action based upon the assumption that most employees 5.____
   A. have an inherent dislike of work
   B. wish to be closely directed
   C. are more interested in security than in assuming responsibility
   D. will exercise self-direction without coercion

6. When there are conflicts or tensions between top management and lower-level employees in any department, the supervisor should FIRST attempt to 6.____
   A. represent and enforce the management point of view
   B. act as the representative of the workers to get their ideas across to management
   C. serve as a two-way spokesman, trying to interpret each side to the other
   D. remain neutral, but keep informed of changes in the situation

7. A probationary period for new employees is usually provided in many agencies. The MAJOR purpose of such a period is usually to 7.____
   A. allow a determination of employee's suitability for the position
   B. obtain evidence as to employee's ability to perform in a higher position
   C. conform to requirements that ethnic hiring goals be met for all positions
   D. train the new employee in the duties of the position

8. An effective program of orientation for new employees usually includes all of the following EXCEPT 8.____
   A. having the supervisor introduce the new employee to his job, outlining his responsibilities and how to carry them out
   B. permitting the new worker to tour the facility or department so he can observe all parts of it in action
   C. scheduling meetings for new employees, at which the job requirements are explained to them and they are given personnel manuals
   D. testing the new worker on his skills and sending him to a centralized in-service workshop

9. In-service training is an important responsibility of many supervisors. The MAJOR reason for such training is to 9.____
   A. avoid future grievance procedures because employees might say they were not prepared to carry out their jobs
   B. maximize the effectiveness of the department by helping each employee perform at his full potential
   C. satisfy inspection teams from central headquarters of the department
   D. help prevent disagreements with members of the community

10. There are many forms of useful in-service training. Of the following, the training method which is NOT an appropriate technique for leadership development is to 10.____
   A. provide special workshops or clinics in activity skills
   B. conduct institutes to familiarize new workers with the program of the department and with their roles

C. schedule team meetings for problem-solving, including both supervisors and leaders
D. have the leader rate himself on an evaluation form periodically

11. Of the following techniques of evaluating work training programs, the one that is BEST is to 11.____
A. pass out a carefully designed questionnaire to the trainees at the completion of the program
B. test the knowledge that trainees have both at the beginning of training and at its completion
C. interview the trainees at the completion of the program
D. evaluate performance before and after training for both a control group and an experimental group

12. Assume that a new supervisor is having difficulty making his instructions to subordinates clearly understood. 12.____
The one of the following which is the FIRST step he should take in dealing with this problem is to
A. set up a training workshop in communication skills
B. determine the extent and nature of the communications gap
C. repeat both verbal and written instructions several times
D. simplify his written and spoken vocabulary

13. A director has not properly carried out the orders of his assistant supervisor on several occasions to the point where he has been successively warned, reprimanded, and severely reprimanded. 13.____
When the director once again does not carry out orders, the PROPER action for the assistant supervisor to take is to
A. bring the director up on charges of failing to perform his duties properly
B. have a serious discussion with the director, explaining the need for the orders and the necessity for carrying them out
C. recommend that the director be transferred to another district
D. severely reprimand the director again, making clear that no further deviation will be countenanced

14. A supervisor with several subordinates becomes aware that two of these subordinates are neither friendly nor congenial. 14.____
In making assignments, it would be BEST for the supervisor to
A. disregard the situation
B. disregard the situation in making a choice of assignment but emphasize the need for teamwork
C. investigate the situation to find out who is at fault and give that individual the less desirable assignments until such time as he corrects his attitude
D. place the unfriendly subordinates in positions where they have as little contact with one another as possible

15. A DESIRABLE characteristic of a good supervisor is that he should 15.____
    A. identify himself with his subordinates rather than with higher management
    B. inform subordinates of forthcoming changes in policies and programs only when they directly affect the subordinates' activities
    C. make advancement of the subordinates contingent on personal loyalty to the supervisor
    D. make promises to subordinates only when sure of the ability to keep them

16. The supervisor who is MOST likely to be successful is the one who 16.____
    A. refrains from exercising the special privileges of his position
    B. maintains a formal attitude toward his subordinates
    C. maintains an informal attitude toward his subordinates
    D. represents the desires of his subordinate to his superiors

17. Application of sound principles of human relations by a supervisor may be expected to _____ the need for formal discipline. 17.____
    A. decrease
    B. have no effect on
    C. increase
    D. obviate

18. The MOST important generally approved way to maintain or develop high morale in one's subordinates is to 18.____
    A. give warnings and reprimands in a jocular way
    B. excuse from staff conferences those employees who are busy
    C. keep them informed of new developments and policies of higher management
    D. refrain from criticizing their faults directly

19. In training subordinates, an IMPORTANT principle for the supervisor to recognize is that 19.____
    A. a particular method of instruction will be of substantially equal value for all employees in a given title
    B. it is difficult to train people over 50 years of age because they have little capacity for learning
    C. persons undergoing the same course of training will learn at different rates of speed
    D. training can seldom achieve its purpose unless individual instruction is the chief method used

20. Over an extended period of time, a subordinate is MOST likely to become and remain most productive if the supervisor 20.____
    A. accords praise to the subordinate whenever his work is satisfactory, withholding criticism except in the case of very inferior work
    B. avoids both praise and criticism except for outstandingly good or bad work performed by the subordinate
    C. informs the subordinate of his shortcomings, as viewed by management, while according praise only when highly deserved
    D. keeps the subordinate informed of the degree of satisfaction with which his performance of the job is viewed by management.

KEY (CORRECT ANSWERS)

1.	C	11.	D
2.	D	12.	B
3.	C	13.	A
4.	A	14.	D
5.	D	15.	D
6.	C	16.	D
7.	A	17.	A
8.	D	18.	C
9.	B	19.	C
10.	D	20.	D

TEST 2

DIRECTIONS: Each question or incomplete statement is followed by several suggested answers or completions. Select the one that BEST answers the question or completes the statement. *PRINT THE LETTER OF THE CORRECT ANSWER IN THE SPACE AT THE RIGHT.*

1. A supervisor has just been told by a subordinate, Mr. Jones, that another employee, Mr. Smith, deliberately disobeyed an important rule of the department by taking home some confidential departmental material. 1.____
Of the following courses of action, it would be MOST advisable for the supervisor FIRST to
   A. discuss the matter privately with both Mr. Jones and Mrs. Smith at the same time
   B. call a meeting of the entire staff and discuss the matter generally without mentioning any employee by name
   C. arrange to supervise Mr. Smith's activities more closely
   D. discuss the matter privately with Mr. Smith

2. The one of the following actions which would be MOST efficient and economical for a supervisor to take to minimize the effect of periodical fluctuations in the workload of his unit is to 2.____
   A. increase his permanent staff until it is large enough to handle the work of the busy loads
   B. request the purchase of time- and labor-saving equipment to be used primarily during the busy loads
   C. lower, temporarily, the standards for quality of work performance during peak loads
   D. schedule for the slow periods work that is not essential to perform during the busy periods

3. Discipline of employees is usually a supervisor's responsibility. There may be several useful forms of disciplinary action. 3.____
Of the following, the form that is LEAST appropriate is the
   A. written reprimand or warning
   B. involuntary transfer to another work setting
   C. demotion or suspension
   D. assignment of added hours of work each week

4. Of the following, the MOST effective means of dealing with employee disciplinary problems is to 4.____
   A. give personality tests to individuals to identify their psychological problems
   B. distribute and discuss a policy manual containing exact rules governing employee behavior
   C. establish a single, clear penalty to be imposed for all wrongdoing irrespective of degree
   D. have supervisors get to know employees well through social mingling

5. A recently developed technique for appraising work performance is to have the supervisor record on a continual basis all significant incidents in each subordinate's behavior that indicate unsuccessful action and those that indicate poor behavior.
Of the following, a MAJOR disadvantage of this method of performance appraisal is that it 5.____
   A. often leads to overly close supervision
   B. results in competition among those subordinates being evaluated
   C. tends to result in superficial judgments
   D. lacks objectivity for evaluating performance

6. Assume that you are a supervisor and have observed the performance of an employee during a period of time. You have concluded that his performance needs improvement.
In order to improve his performance, it would, therefore, be BEST for you to 6.____
   A. note your findings in the employee's personnel folder so that his behavior is a matter of record
   B. report the findings to the personnel officer so he can take prompt action
   C. schedule a problem-solving conference with the employee
   D. recommend his transfer to simpler duties

7. When an employee's absences or latenesses seem to be nearing excessiveness, the supervisor should speak with him to find out what the problem is.
Of the following, if such a discussion produces no reasonable explanation, the discussion usually BEST serves to 7.____
   A. affirm clearly the supervisor's adherence to proper policy
   B. alert other employees that such behavior is unacceptable
   C. demonstrate that the supervisor truly represents higher management
   D. notify the employee that his behavior is being observed and evaluated

8. Assume that an employee willfully and recklessly violates an important agency regulation. The nature of the violation is of such magnitude that it demands immediate action, but the facts of the case are not entirely clear. Further, assume that the supervisor is free to make any of the following recommendations.
The MOST appropriate action for the supervisor to take is to recommend that the employee be 8.____
   A. discharged B. suspended
   C. forced to resign D. transferred

9. Although employees' titles may be identical, each position in that title may be considerably different.
Of the following, a supervisor should carefully assign each employee to a specific position based PRIMARILY on the employee's 9.____
   A. capability B. experience C. education D. seniority

10. The one of the following situations where it is MOST appropriate to transfer an employee to a similar assignment is one in which the employee 10.____
    A. lacks motivation and interest
    B. experiences a personality conflict with his supervisor
    C. is negligent in the performance of his duties
    D. lacks capacity or ability to perform assigned tasks

11. The one of the following which is LEAST likely to be affected by improvements in the morale of personnel is employee 11.____
    A. skill
    B. absenteeism
    C. turnover
    D. job satisfaction

12. The one of the following situations in which it is LEAST appropriate for a supervisor to delegate authority to subordinates is where the supervisor 12.____
    A. lacks confidence in his own abilities to perform certain work
    B. is overburdened and cannot handle all his responsibilities
    C. refers all disciplinary problems to his subordinate
    D. has to deal with an emergency or crisis

13. Assume that it has come to your attention that two of your subordinates have shouted at each other and have almost engaged in a fist fight. Luckily, they were separated by some of the other employees. 13.____
    Of the following, your BEST immediate course of action would generally be to
    A. reprimand the senior of the two subordinates since he should have known better
    B. hear the story from both employees and any witnesses and then take needed disciplinary action
    C. ignore the matter since nobody was physically hurt
    D. immediately suspend and fine both employees pending a departmental hearing

14. You have been delegating some of your authority to one of your subordinates because of his leadership potential. 14.____
    Which of the following actions is LEAST conducive to the growth and development of this individual for a supervisory position?
    A. Use praise only when it will be effective
    B. Give very detailed instructions and supervise the employee closely to be sure that the instructions ae followed precisely
    C. Let the subordinate proceed with his planned course of action even if mistakes, within a permissible range, are made
    D. Intervene on behalf of the subordinate whenever an assignment becomes difficult for him

15. A rumor has been spreading in your department concerning the possibility of layoffs due to decreased revenues. 15.____
    As a supervisor, you should GENERALLY
    A. deny the rumor, whether it is true or false, in order to keep morale from declining

B. inform the men to the best of your knowledge about this situation and keep them advised of any new information
C. tell the men to forget about the rumor and concentrate on increasing their productivity
D. ignore the rumor since it is not authorized information

16. Within an organization, every supervisor should know to whom he reports and who reports to him. 16.____
The one of the following which is achieved by use of such structured relationships is
A. unity of command
B. confidentiality
C. esprit de corps
D. promotion opportunities

17. Almost every afternoon, one of your employees comes back from his break ten minutes late without giving you any explanation. 17.____
Which of the following actions should you take FIRST in this situation?
A. Assign the employee to a different type of work and observe whether his behavior changes
B. Give the employee extra work to do so that he will have to return on time
C. Ask the employee for an explanation for his lateness
D. Tell the employee he is jeopardizing the break for everyone

18. When giving instructions to your employees in a group, which one of the following should you make certain to do? 18.____
A. Speak in a casual, off-hand manner
B. Assume that your employees fully understand the instructions
C. Write out your instructions beforehand and read them to the employees
D. Tell exactly who is to do what

19. A fist fight develops between two men under your supervision. 19.____
The MOST advisable course of action for you to take FIRST is to
A. call the police
B. have the other workers pull them apart
C. order them to stop
D. step between the two men

20. You have assigned some difficult and unusual work to one of your most experienced and competent subordinates. 20.____
If you notice that he is doing the work incorrectly, you should
A. assign the work to another employee
B. reprimand him in private
C. show him immediately how the work should be done
D. wait until the job is completed and then correct his errors

KEY (CORRECT ANSWERS)

1.	D	11.	A
2.	D	12.	C
3.	D	13.	B
4.	B	14.	B
5.	A	15.	B
6.	C	16.	A
7.	D	17.	C
8.	B	18.	D
9.	A	19.	C
10.	B	20.	C

SUPERVISION, ADMINISTRATION, MANAGEMENT AND ORGANIZATION

EXAMINATION SECTION

TEST 1

DIRECTIONS: Each question or incomplete statement is followed by several suggested answers or completions. Select the one that BEST answers the question or completes the statement. *PRINT THE LETTER OF THE CORRECT ANSWER IN THE SPACE AT THE RIGHT.*

1. The one of the following situations in which you as a supervisor of a group of clerks would probably be able to function MOST effectively from the viewpoint of departmental efficiency is where you are responsible DIRECTLY to 1.____
   A. a single supervisor having sole jurisdiction over you
   B. two or three supervisors having coordinate jurisdiction over you
   C. four or five supervisors having coordinate jurisdiction over you
   D. all individuals of higher rank than you in the department

2. Suppose that it is necessary to order one of the clerks under your supervision to stay overtime a few hours one evening. The work to be done is not especially difficult. It is the custom in your office to make such assignments by rotation. The particular clerk whose turn it is to work overtime requests to be excused that evening, but offers to work the next time that overtime is necessary. Hitherto, this clerk has always been very cooperative. 2.____
   Of the following, the BEST action for you to take is to
   A. grant the clerk's request, but require her to work overtime two additional nights to compensate for this concession
   B. inform the clerk that you are compelled to refuse any request for special consideration
   C. grant the clerk's request if another clerk is willing to substitute for her
   D. refuse the clerk's request outright because granting her request may encourage her to evade other responsibilities

3. When asked to comment upon the efficiency of Miss Jones, a clerk, her supervisor said, "Since she rarely makes an error, I consider her very efficient." 3.____
   Of the following, the MOST valid assumption underlying this supervisor's comment is that
   A. speed and accuracy should be considered separately in evaluating a clerk's efficiency
   B. the most accurate clerks are not necessarily the most efficient
   C. accuracy and competency are directly related
   D. accuracy is largely dependent upon the intelligence of a clerk

4. The one of the following which is the MOST accurate statement of one of the functions of a supervisor is to 4.____
   A. select scientifically the person best fitted for the specific job to be done
   B. train the clerks assigned to you in the best methods of doing the work of your office
   C. fit the job to be done to the clerks who are available
   D. assign a clerk only to those tasks for which she has the necessary experience

5. Assume that you, an experienced supervisor, are given a newly appointed clerk to assist you in performing a certain task. The new clerk presents a method of doing the task which is different from your method but which is obviously better and easy to adopt. 5.____
Of the following you, the supervisor, should
   A. take the suggestion and try it out, even though it was offered by someone less experienced
   B. reject the idea, even though it appears an improvement, as it very likely would not work out
   C. send the new clerk away and get someone else to assist who will be more in accord with your ideas
   D. report him to the head of the office and ask that the new clerk be instructed to do things your way

6. As a supervisor, you should realize that the one of the following general abilities of a junior clerk which is probably LEAST susceptible to improvement by practice and training is 6.____
   A. intelligence
   B. speed of typing
   C. knowledge of office procedures
   D. accuracy of filing

7. As a supervisor, when training an employee, you should NOT 7.____
   A. correct errors as he makes them
   B. give him too much material to absorb at one time
   C. have him try the operation until he can do it perfectly
   D. treat any foolish question seriously

8. If a supervisor cannot check readily all the work in her unit, she should 8.____
   A. hold up the work until she can personally check it
   B. refuse to take additional work
   C. work overtime until she can personally finish it
   D. delegate part of the work to a qualified subordinate

9. The one of the following over which a unit supervisor has the LEAST control is 9.____
   A. the quality of the work done in his unit
   B. the nature of the work handled in his unit
   C. the morale of workers in his unit
   D. increasing efficiency of his unit

10. Suppose that you have received a note from an important official in your department commending the work of a unit of clerks under your supervision. Of the following, the BEST action for you to take is to 10.____
   A. withhold the note for possible use at a time when the morale of the unit appears to be declining
   B. show the note only to the better members of your staff as a reward for their good work
   C. show the note only to the poorer members of your staff as a stimulus for better work
   D. post the note conspicuously so that it can be seen by all members of your staff

11. If you find that one of your subordinates is becoming apathetic towards his work, you should 11.____
   A. prefer charges against him
   B. change the type of work
   C. request his transfer
   D. advise him to take a medical examination to check his health

12. Suppose that a new clerk has been assigned to the unit which you supervise. To give this clerk a brief picture of the functioning of your unit in the entire department would be 12.____
   A. *commendable*, because she will probably be able to perform her work with more understanding
   B. *undesirable*, because such action will probably serve only to confuse her
   C. *commendable*, because, if transferred, she would probably be able to work efficiently without additional training
   D. *undesirable*, because in-service training has been demonstrated to be less efficient than on-the-job training

13. Written instructions to a subordinate are of value because they 13.____
   A. can be kept up-to-date
   B. encourage initiative
   C. make a job seem easier
   D. are an aid in training

14. Suppose that you have assigned a task to a clerk under your supervision and have given appropriate instructions. After a reasonable period, you check her work and find that one specific aspect of her work is consistently incorrect. Of the following, the BEST action for you to take is to 14.____
   A. determine whether the clerk has correctly understood instructions concerning the aspect of the work not being done correctly
   B. assign the task to a more competent clerk
   C. wait for the clerk to commit a more flagrant error before taking up the matter with her
   D. indicate to the clerk that you are dissatisfied with her work and wait to see whether she is sufficiently intelligent to correct her own mistakes

15. If you wanted to check on the accuracy of the filing in your unit, you would 15.____
    A. check all the files thoroughly at regular intervals
    B. watch the clerks while they are filing
    C. glance through filed papers at random
    D. inspect thoroughly a small section of the files selected at random

16. In making job assignments to his subordinates, a supervisor should follow the principle that each individual generally is capable of 16.____
    A. performing one type of work well and less capable of performing other types well
    B. learning to perform a wide variety of different types of work
    C. performing best the type of work in which he has had least experience
    D. learning to perform any type of work in which he is given training

17. Of the following, the information that is generally considered MOST essential in a departmental organization survey chart is the 17.____
    A. detailed operations of the department
    B. lines of authority
    C. relations of the department to other departments
    D. names of the employees of the department

18. Suppose you are the supervisor in charge of a large unit in which all of the clerical staff perform similar tasks. 18.____
    In evaluating the relative accuracy of the clerks, the clerk who should be considered to be the LEAST accurate is the one
    A. whose errors result in the greatest financial loss
    B. whose errors cost the most to locate
    C. who makes the greatest percentage of errors in his work
    D. who makes the greatest number of errors in the unit

19. Aside from requirements imposed by authority, the frequency with which reports are submitted or the length of the interval which they cover should depend PRINCIPALLY on the 19.____
    A. availability of the data to be included in the reports
    B. amount of time required to prepare the reports
    C. extent of the variations in the data with the passage of time
    D. degree of comprehensiveness required in the reports

20. A serious error has been discovered by a critical superior in work carried on under your supervision. 20.____
    It is BEST to explain the situation and prevent its recurrence by
    A. claiming that you are not responsible because you do not check the work personally
    B. accepting the complaint and reporting the name of the employee responsible for the error
    C. assuring him that you hope it will not occur again
    D. assuring him that you will find out how it occurred, so that you can have the work checked with greater care in the future

21. A serious procedural problem develops in your office. 21.____
In your solution of this problem, the very FIRST step to take is to
   A. select the personnel to help you
   B. analyze your problem
   C. devise the one best method of research
   D. develop an outline of your report

22. Your office staff consists of eight clerks, stenographers, and typists, cramped in a long narrow room. The room is very difficult to ventilate properly, and, as in so many other offices, the disagreement over the method of ventilation is marked. Two cliques are developing and the friction is carrying over into the work of the office. 22.____
Of the following, the BEST way to proceed is to
   A. call your staff together, have the matter fully discussed giving each person an opportunity to be heard, and put the matter to a vote; then enforce the method of ventilation which has the most votes
   B. call your staff together and have the matter fully discussed. If a compromise arrangement is agreed upon, put it into effect. Otherwise, on the basis of all the facts at your disposal, make a decision as to how best to ventilate the room and enforce your decision
   C. speak to the employees individually, make a decision as to how to ventilate the room, and then enforce your decision
   D. study the layout of the office, make a decision as to how best to ventilate the room, and then enforce your decision

23. An organization consisting of six levels of authority, where eight persons are assigned to each supervisor on each level, would consist of APPROXIMATELY _____ persons. 23.____
   A. 50 B. 500 C. 5,000 D. 50,000

24. The one of the following which is considered by political scientists to be a GOOD principle of municipal government is 24.____
   A. concentration of authority and responsibility
   B. the long ballot
   C. low salaries and a narrow range in salaries
   D. short terms for elected city officials

25. Of the following, the statement concerning the organization of a department which is TRUE is: 25.____
   A. In general, no one employee should have active and constant supervision over more than ten persons.
   B. It is basically unwise to have a supervisor with only three subordinates.
   C. It is desirable that there be no personal contact between the rank and file employee and the supervisor once removed from him.
   D. There should be no more than four levels of authority between the top administrative office in a department and the rank and file employees.

26. Assuming that Dictaphones are not available, of the following, the situation in which it would be MOST desirable to establish a central stenographic unit is one in which the unit would serve 26.____
    A. ten correspondence clerks assigned to full-time positions answering correspondence of a large government department
    B. seven members of a government commission heading a large department
    C. seven heads of bureaus in a government department consisting of 250 employees
    D. fifty investigators in a large department

27. You are assigned to review the procedures in an office in order to recommend improvements to the commissioner directly. You go into an office performing seen routine operations in the processing of one type of office form. The question you should FIRST ask yourself in your study of any one of these operations is: 27.____
    A. Can it be simplified?
    B. Is it necessary?
    C. Is it performed in proper order or should its position in the procedure be changed?
    D. Is the equipment for doing it satisfactory?

28. You are assigned in charge of a clerical bureau performing a single operation. All five of your subordinates do exactly the same work. A fine spirit of cooperation has developed and the employees help each other and pool their completed work so that the work of any one employee is indistinguishable. Your office is very busy and all five clerks are doing a full day's work. However, reports come back to you from other offices that they are finding as much as 1% error in the work of your bureau. This is too high a percentage of error. Of the following, the BEST procedure for you to follow is to 28.____
    A. check all the work yourself
    B. have a sample of the work of each clerk checked by another clerk
    C. have all work done in your office checked by one of your clerks
    D. identify the work of each clerk in some way

29. You are put in charge of a small office. In order to cover the office during the lunch hour, you assign Employee A to remain in the office between the hours of 12 and 1 P.M. On your return to the office at 12:25 P.M., you note that no one is in the office and that the phone is ringing. You are forced to postpone your 12:30 P.M. luncheon appointment, and to remain in the office until 12:50 P.M. when Employee A returns to the office. The BEST of the following actions is: 29.____
    A. Ask Employee why he left the office
    B. Bring charges against Employee A for insubordination and neglect of duty
    C. Ignore the matter in your conversation with Employee A so as not to embarrass him
    D. Make a note to rate Employee A low on his service rating

30. You are assigned in charge of a large division. It had been the practice in that division for the employees to slip out for breakfast about 10:00 A.M. You had been successful in stopping this practice and for one week no one had gone out for breakfast. One day a stenographer comes over to you at 10:30 A.M. appearing to be ill. She states that she doesn't feel well and that she would like to go out for a cup of tea. She asks your permission to leave the office for a few minutes. 30.____
You should
   A. telephone and have a cup of tea delivered to her
   B. permit her to go out
   C. refuse her permission to go out inasmuch as this would be setting a bad example
   D. tell her she can leave for an early lunch hour

31. The following four remarks from a supervisor to a subordinate deal with different situations. One remark, however, implies a basically POOR supervisory practice. 31.____
Select this remark as your answer.
   A. "I've called the staff together primarily because I am displeased with the work which one of you is doing. John, don't you think you should be ashamed that you are spoiling the good work of the office?"
   B. "James, you have been with us for six months now. In general, I'm satisfied with your work. However, don't you think you could be more neat in your appearance? I also want you to try to be more accurate in your work."
   C. "Joe, when I assigned this job to you, I did it because it requires special care and I think you're one of our best men in this type of work, but here is a slip-up you've made that we should be especially careful to watch out for in the future."
   D. "Tim, first I'd like to tell you that, effective tomorrow, you are to be my assistant and will receive an increase in salary. Although I recommended you for this position because I felt that you are the best man for the job, there are some things about your work which could stand a bit of improvement. For instance, your manner with regard to visitors is not so polite as it could be."

32. Of the following, the BEST type of floor surface for an office is 32.____
   A. concrete   B. hardwood   C. linoleum   D. parquet

33. The GENERALLY accepted unit for the measurement of illumination at a desk or work bench is the 33.____
   A. ampere   B. foot-candle   C. volt   D. watt

34. The one of the following who is MOST closely allied with "scientific management" is 34.____
   A. Mosher   B. Probst   C. Taylor   D. White

35. Eliminating slack in work assignments is 35.____
   A. speed-up
   B. time study
   C. motion study
   D. efficient management

36. "Time studies" examine and measure 36.____
   A. past performance
   B. present performance
   C. long-run effect
   D. influence of change

37. The maximum number of subordinates who can be effectively supervised by one supervisor is BEST considered as 37.____
   A. determined by the law of "span of control"
   B. determined by the law of "span of attention"
   C. determined by the type of work supervised
   D. fixed at not more than six

38. In the theory and practice of public administration, the one of the following which is LEAST generally regarded as a staff function is 38.____
   A. budgeting
   B. firefighting
   C. purchasing
   D. research and information

39. Suppose you are part of an administrative structure in which the executive head has regularly reporting directly to him seventeen subordinates. To some of the subordinates there regularly report directly three employees, to others four employees, and to the remaining subordinates five employees. 39.____
Called upon to make a suggestion concerning this organization, you would question FIRST the desirability of
   A. so large a variation among the number of employees regularly reporting directly to subordinates
   B. having so large a number of subordinates regularly reporting directly to the administrative head
   C. so small a variation among the number of employees regularly reporting directly to subordinates
   D. the hierarchical arrangement

40. Administration is the center but not necessarily the source of all ideas for procedural improvement. 40.____
The MOST significant implication that this principle bears for the administrative officer is that
   A. before procedural improvements are introduced, they should be approved by a majority of the staff
   B. it is the unique function of the administrative officer to derive and introduce procedural improvements
   C. the administrative office should derive ideas and suggestions for procedural improvement from all possible sources, introducing any that promise to be effective
   D. the administrative officer should view employee grievances as the chief source of procedural improvements

41. The merit system should not end with the appointment of a candidate. In any worthy public service system there should be no dead-end jobs. If the best citizen is to be attracted to public service, there must be provided encouragement and incentive to enable such a career employee to progress in the service. 41.____
The one of the following which is the MOST accurate statement on the basis of the above statement is that
   A. merit system selection has replaced political appointment in many governmental units
   B. lack of opportunities for advancement in government employment will discourage the better qualified from applying
   C. employees who want to progress in the public service should avoid simple assignments
   D. most dead-end jobs have been eliminated from the public service

42. Frequently the importance of keeping office records is not appreciated until information which is badly needed cannot be found. Office records must be kept in convenient and legible form, and must be filed where they may be found quickly. Many clerks are required for this work in large offices and fixed standards of accomplishment often can and must be utilized to get the desired results without loss of time. 42.____
The one of the following which is the MOST accurate statement on the basis of the above statement is:
   A. In setting up a filing system, the system to be used is secondary to the purpose it is to serve.
   B. Office records to be valuable must be kept in duplicate.
   C. The application of work standards to certain clerical functions frequently leads to greater efficiency.
   D. The keeping of office records becomes increasingly important as the business transacted by an office grows.

43. The difference between the average worker and the expert in any occupation is to a large degree a matter of training, yet the difference in their output is enormous. Despite this fact, there are many offices which do not have any organized system of training. 43.____
The MOST accurate of the following statements on the basis of the above statement is that
   A. job training, to be valuable, should be a continuous process
   B. most clerks have the same general intelligence but differ only in the amount of training they have received
   C. skill in an occupation can be acquired as a result of instruction by others
   D. employees with similar training will produce similar quality and quantity of work

44. Sometimes the term "clerical work" is used synonymously with the term "office work" to indicate that the work is clerical work, whether done by a clerk in a place called "the office," by the foreman in the shop, or by an investigator in the field. The essential feature is the work itself, not who does it or where it is done. If it is clerical work in one place, it is clerical work everywhere. 44.____

Of the following, the LEAST DIRECT implication of the above statement is that
- A. many jobs have clerical aspects
- B. some clerical work is done in offices
- C. the term "clerical work" is used in place of the term "office work" to emphasize the nature of the work done rather than by whom it is done
- D. clerks are not called upon to perform other than clerical work

45. Scheduling work within a unit involves the knowledge of how long the component parts of the routine take, and the precedence which certain routines should take over others. Usually, the important functions should be attended to on a schedule, and less important work can be handled as fill-in. 45.____
The one of the following which is the VALID statement on the basis of the above statement is that
- A. only employees engaged in routine assignments should have their work scheduled
- B. the work of an employee should be so scheduled that occasional absences will not upset his routine
- C. a proper scheduling of work takes the importance of the various functions of a unit into consideration
- D. if office work is not properly scheduled, important functions will be neglected

46. A filing system is unquestionably an effective tool for the systematic executive, and it use in office practice is indispensable, but a casual examination of almost any filing drawer in any office will show that hundreds of letters and papers which have no value whatever are being preserved. 46.____
The LEAST accurate of the following statements on the basis of the above statement is that
- A. it is generally considered to be good office practice to destroy letters or papers which are of no value
- B. many files are cluttered with useless paper
- C. a filing system is a valuable aid in effective office management
- D. every office executive should personally make a thorough examination of the files at regular intervals

47. As a supervisor, you may receive requests for information which you know should not be divulged. 47.____
Of the following replies you may give to such a request received over the telephone, the BEST one is:
- A. "I regret to advise you that it is the policy of the department not to give out this information over the telephone."
- B. "If you hold on a moment, I'll have you connected with the chief of the division."
- C. "I am sorry that I cannot help you, but we are not permitted to give out any information regarding such matters."
- D. "I am sorry but I know nothing regarding this matter."

48. Training promotes cooperation and teamwork, and results in lowered unit costs of operation. 48.____
The one of the following which is the MOST valid implication of the above statement is that
   A. training is of most value to new employees
   B. training is a factor in increasing efficiency and morale
   C. the actual cost of training employees may be small
   D. training is unnecessary in offices where personnel costs cannot be reduced

49. A government employee should understand how his particular duties contribute to the achievement of the objectives of his department. 49.____
This statement means MOST NEARLY that
   A. an employee who understands the functions of his department will perform his work efficiently
   B. all employees contribute equally in carrying out the objectives of their department
   C. an employee should realize the significance of his work in relation to the aims of his department
   D. all employees should be able to assist in setting up the objectives of a department

50. Many office managers have a tendency to overuse form letters and are prone to print form letters for every occasion, regardless of the number of copies of these letters which is needed. 50.____
On the basis of this statement, it is MOST logical to state that the determination of the need for a form letter should depend upon the
   A. length of the period during which the form letter may be used
   B. number of form letters presently being used in the office
   C. frequency with which the form letter may be used
   D. number of typists who may use the form letter

KEY (CORRECT ANSWERS)

1.	A	11.	B	21.	B	31.	A	41.	B
2.	C	12.	A	22.	B	32.	C	42.	C
3.	C	13.	D	23.	A	33.	B	43.	C
4.	B	14.	A	24.	A	34.	C	44.	D
5.	A	15.	D	25.	D	35.	D	45.	C
6.	A	16.	B	26.	D	36.	B	46.	D
7.	B	17.	B	27.	B	37.	C	47.	C
8.	D	18.	C	28.	D	38.	B	48.	B
9.	B	19.	C	29.	A	39.	B	49.	C
10.	D	20.	D	30.	B	40.	C	50.	C

TEST 2

DIRECTIONS: Each question or incomplete statement is followed by several suggested answers or completions. Select the one that BEST answers the question or completes the statement. *PRINT THE LETTER OF THE CORRECT ANSWER IN THE SPACE AT THE RIGHT.*

1. Your bureau is assigned an important task. 1.____
Of the following, the function that you, as an administrative officer, can LEAST reasonably be expected to perform under these circumstances is the
   A. division of the large job into individual tasks
   B. establishment of "production lines" within the bureau
   C. performance personally of a substantial share of all the work
   D. checkup to see that the work has been well done

2. Suppose that you have broken a complex job into its smaller components before making assignments to the employees under your jurisdiction. 2.____
Of the following, the LEAST advisable procedure to follow from that point is to
   A. give each employee a picture of the importance of his work for the success of the total job
   B. establish a definite line of work flow and responsibility
   C. post a written memorandum of the best method for performing each job
   D. teach a number of alternative methods for doing each job

3. As an administrative officer, you are requested to draw up an organization chart of the whole department. 3.____
Of the following, the MOST important characteristic of such a chart is that it will
   A. include all details of the organization which distinguish it from any other
   B. be a schematic representation of purely administrative functions within the department
   C. present a modification of the actual departmental organization in light of principles of scientific management
   D. present an accurate picture of the lines of authority and responsibility

4. Of the following, the MOST important principle in respect to delegation of authority that should guide you in your work as supervisor in charge of a bureau is that you should 4.____
   A. delegate as much authority as you effectively can
   B. make certain that all administrative details clear through your desk
   C. have all decisions confirmed by you
   D. discourage the practice of consulting you on matters of basic policy

5. Of the following, the LEAST valid criterion to be applied in evaluating the organization of the department in which you are employed as a supervisor is: 5.____
   A. Is authority for making decisions centralized?
   B. Is authority for formulating policy centralized?
   C. Is authority granted commensurate with the responsibility involved?
   D. Is each position and its relation to other positions from the standpoint of responsibility clearly defined?

6. Functional centralization is the bringing together of employees doing the same kind of work and performing similar tasks. 6.____
Of the following, the one which is NOT an important advantage flowing from the introduction of functional centralization in a large city department is that
   A. inter-bureau communication and traffic are reduced
   B. standardized work procedures are introduced more easily
   C. evaluation of employee performances is facilitated
   D. inequalities in working conditions are reduced

7. As a supervisor, you find that a probationary employee under your supervision is consistently below a reasonable standard of performance for the job he is assigned to do. 7.____
Of the following, the MOST appropriate action for you to take FIRST is to
   A. give him an easier job to do
   B. advise him to transfer to another department
   C. recommend to your superior that he be discouraged at the end of his probationary period
   D. determine whether the cause for his below-standard performance can be readily remedied

8. Certain administrative functions, such as those concerned with budgetary and personnel selection activities, have been delegated to central agencies separated from the operating departments. 8.____
Of the following, the PRINCIPAL reason for such separation is that
   A. a central agency is generally better able to secure funds for performing these functions
   B. decentralization increases executive control
   C. greater economy, efficiency, and uniformity can be obtained by establishing central staff of experts to perform these functions
   D. the problems involved in performing these functions vary significantly from one operating department to another

9. The one of the following which is LEAST valid as a guiding principle for you, in your work as supervisor, in building team spirit and teamwork in your bureau is that you should attempt to 9.____
   A. convince the personnel of the bureau that public administration is a worthwhile endeavor
   B. lead every employee to visualize the integration of his own individual function with the program of the whole bureau
   C. develop a favorable public attitude toward the work of the bureau
   D. maintain impartiality by convenient delegation of authority in controversial matters

10. Of the following, the LEAST desirable procedure for the competent supervisor to follow is to 10.____
   A. organize his work before taking responsibility for helping others with theirs
   B. avoid schedules and routines when he is busy
   C. be flexible in planning and carrying out his responsibilities
   D. secure the support of his staff in organizing the total job of the unit

11. The responsibility for making judgment about staff members which is inherent in the supervisor's position may arouse hostilities toward the supervisor. 11.____
Of the following, the BEST suggestion to the supervisor for handling this responsibility is for the supervisor to avoid
   A. individual criticism by taking up problems directly through group meetings
   B. any personal feeling or action that would imply that the supervisor has any power over the staff
   C. making critical judgments without accompanying them with reassurance to the staff member concerned

12. To carry out MOST effectively his responsibility for holding to a standard of quantity and quality, the supervisor should 12.____
   A. demand much more from himself than he does from his staff
   B. provide a clearly defined statement of what is expected of the staff
   C. teach the staff to assume responsible attitudes
   D. help the staff out when they get into unavoidable difficulties

13. The supervisor should inspire confidence and respect. 13.____
This objective is MOST likely to be attained by the supervisor if he endeavors always to
   A. know the answers to the workers' questions
   B. be fair and just
   C. know what is going on in the office
   D. behave like a supervisor

14. Two chief reasons for the centralization of office functions are to eliminate costly duplication and to bring about greater coordination. 14.____
The MOST direct implication of this statement is that
   A. greater coordination of office work will result in centralization of office functions
   B. where there is no centralization of office functions, there can be no coordination of work
   C. centralization of office functions may reduce duplication of work
   D. decentralization of office functions may be a result of costly duplication

15. The efficient administrative assistant arranges a definite schedule of the regular work of his division, but assigns the occasional and emergency tasks when they arise to the employees available at the time to handle these tasks. 15.____
The management procedure described in this statement is desirable MAINLY because it
   A. relieves the administrative assistant of the responsibility of supervising the work of his staff
   B. enables more of the staff to become experienced in handling different types of problems
   C. enables the administrative assistant to anticipate problems which may arise
   D. provides for consideration of current work load when making special assignments

16. Well-organized training courses for office employees are regarded by most administrators as a fundamental and essential part of a well-balanced personnel program. 16.____
Such training of clerical employees results LEAST directly in
   A. providing a reservoir of trained employees who can carry on the duties of other clerks during the absence of these clerks
   B. reducing the individual differences in the innate ability of clerical employees to perform complex duties
   C. bringing about a standardization throughout the department of operational methods found to be highly effective in one of its units
   D. preparing clerical employees for promotion to more responsible positions

17. The average typing speed of a typist is not necessarily a true indication of her efficiency. 17.____
Of the following, the BEST justification for this statement is that
   A. the typist may not maintain her maximum typing speed at all times
   B. a rapid typist will ordinarily type more letters than a slow one
   C. a typist's assignments usually include other operations in addition to actual typing
   D. typing speed has no significant relationship to the difficulty of material being typed

18. Although the use of labor-saving machinery and the simplification of procedures tend to decrease unit clerical labor costs, there is, nevertheless, a contrary tendency in the overall cost of office work. This contrary tendency, evidenced by the increase in size of the office staffs, has developed from the increasingly extensive use of systems of analysis and methods of research. 18.____
Of the following, the MOST accurate statement on the basis of the above statement is that
   A. the tendency for the overall costs of office work to increase is bringing about a counter-tendency to decrease unit costs of office work
   B. office machines are of little value in reducing the unit costs of the work of offices in which the overall costs are increasing
   C. The increasing use of systems of analysis and methods of research is bringing about a condition which will necessitate a curtailment of the use of these techniques in the office
   D. expanded office functions tend to offset savings resulting from increased efficiency in office management

19. The most successful supervisor wins his victories through preventive rather than through curative action. 19.____
The one of the following which is the MOST accurate statement on the basis of this statement is that
   A. success in supervision may be measured more accurately in terms of errors corrected than in terms of errors prevented
   B. anticipating problems makes for better supervision than waiting until these problems arise

C. difficulties that cannot be prevented by the supervisor cannot be overcome
D. the solution of problems in supervision is best achieved by scientific methods

20. Assume that you have been requested to design an office form which is to be duplicated by the mimeograph process. 20.____
In planning the layout of the various items appearing on the form, it is LEAST important for you to know the
A. amount of information which the form is to contain
B. purpose for which the form will be used
C. size of the form
D. number of copies of the form which are required

21. The supervisor is responsible for the accuracy of the work performed by her subordinates. 21.____
Of the following procedures which she might adopt to insure the accurate copying of long reports from rough draft originals, the MOST effective one is to
A. examine the rough draft for errors in grammar, punctuation, and spelling before assigning it to a typist to copy
B. glance through each typed report before it leaves her bureau to detect any obvious errors made by the typist
C. have another employee read the rough draft original to the typist who typed the report, and have the typist make whatever corrections are necessary
D. rotate assignments involving the typing of long reports equally among all the typists in the unit

22. The total number of errors made during the month, or other period studied, indicates, in a general way, whether the work has been performed with reasonable accuracy. However, this is not in itself a true measure, but must be considered in relation to the total volume of work produced. 22.____
On the basis of this statement, the accuracy of work performed is MOST truly measured by the
A. total number of errors made during a specified period
B. comparison of the number of errors made and the quantity of work produced during a specified period
C. average amount of work produced by the unit during each month or other designated period of time
D. none of the above answers

23. In the course of your duties, you receive a letter which, you believe, should be called to the attention of your supervisor. 23.____
Of the following, the BEST reason for attaching previous correspondence to this letter before giving it to your supervisor is that
A. there is less danger, if such a procedure is followed, of misplacing important letters
B. this letter can probably be better understood in the light of previous correspondence

C. your supervisor is probably in a better position to understand the letter than you
D. this letter will have to be filed eventually so there is no additional work involved

24. Suppose that you are requested to transmit to the stenographers in your bureau an order curtailing certain privileges that they have been enjoying. You anticipate that your staff may resent curtailment of such privileges. 24.____
Of the following, the BEST action for you to take is to
A. impress upon your staff that an order is an order and must be obeyed
B. attempt to explain to your staff the probable reasons for curtailing their privileges
C. excuse the curtailment of privileges by saying that the welfare of the staff was evidently not considered
D. warn your staff that violation of an order may be considered sufficient cause for immediate dismissal

25. Suppose that a stenographer recently appointed to your bureau submits a memorandum suggesting a change in office procedure that has been tried before and has been found unsuccessful. 25.____
Of the following, the BEST action for you to take is to
A. send the stenographer a note acknowledging receipt of the suggestion, but do not attempt to carry out the suggestion
B. point out that suggestions should come from her supervisor, who has a better knowledge of the problems of the office
C. try out the suggested change a second time, lest the stenographer lose interest in her work
D. call the stenographer in, explain that the change if not practicable, and compliment her for her interest and alertness

26. Suppose that you are assistant to one of the important administrators in your department. You receive a note from the head of department asking your supervisor to assist with a pressing problem that has arisen by making an immediate recommendation. Your supervisor is out of town on official business for a few days and cannot be reached. The head of department, evidently, is not aware of his absence. 26.____
Of the following, the BEST action for you to take is to
A. send the note back to the head of department without comment so as not to incriminate your supervisor
B. forward the note to one of the administrators in another division of the department
C. wait until your supervisor returns and bring the note to his attention immediately
D. get in touch with the head of department immediately and inform him that your supervisor is out of town

27. One of your duties may be to estimate the budget of your unit for the next fiscal year. Suppose that you expect no important changes in the work of your unit during the next year. 27.____

Of the following, the MOST appropriate basis for estimating next year's budget is the

A. average budget of your unit for the last five years
B. budget of your unit for the current year plus fifty percent to allow for possible expansion
C. average current budget of units in your department
D. budget of your unit for the current fiscal year

28. As a supervisor, you should realize that the work of a stenographer ordinarily requires a higher level of intelligence than the work of a typist CHIEFLY because 28.____

A. the salary range of stenographers is, in most government and business offices, lower than the salary range of typists
B. greater accuracy and skill is ordinarily required of a typist
C. the stenographer must understand what is being dictated to enable her to write it out in shorthand
D. typists are required to do more technical and specialized work

29. Suppose that you are acting as assistant to an important administrator in your department. 29.____
Of the following, the BEST reason for keeping a separate "pending" file of letters to which answers are expected very soon is that

A. important correspondence should be placed in a separate, readily accessible file
B. a periodic check of the "pending" file will indicate the possible need for follow-up letters
C. correspondence is never final, so provision should be made for keeping files open
D. there is seldom sufficient room in the permanent files to permit filing all letters

30. For a busy executive in a government department, the services of an assistant are valuable and almost indispensable. 30.____
Of the following, the CHIEF value of an assistant PROBABLY lies in her

A. ability to assume responsibility for making major decisions
B. familiarity with the general purpose and functions of civil service
C. special education
D. familiarity with the work and detail involved in the duties of the executive whom she assists

31. The supervisor should set a good example. 31.____
Of the following, the CHIEF implication of the above statement is that the supervisor should

A. behave as he expects his workers to behave
B. know as much about the worker as his workers do
C. keep his workers informed of what he is doing
D. keep ahead of his workers

32. Of the following, the LEAST desirable procedure for the competent supervisor to follow is to 32.____
    A. organize his work before taking responsibility for helping others with theirs
    B. avoid schedules and routines when he is busy
    C. be flexible in planning and carrying out his responsibilities
    D. secure the support of his staff in organizing the total job of the unit

33. Evaluation helps the worker by increasing his security. 33.____
Of the following, the BEST justification for this statement is that
    A. security and growth depend upon knowledge by the worker of the agency's evaluation
    B. knowledge of his evaluation by agency and supervisor will stimulate the worker to better performance
    C. evaluation enables the supervisor and worker to determine the reasons for the worker's strengths and weaknesses
    D. the supervisor and worker together can usually recognize and deal with any worker's insecurity

34. Systematizing for efficiency means MOST NEARLY 34.____
    A. performing an assignment despite all interruptions
    B. leaving difficult assignments until the next day
    C. having a definite time schedule for certain daily duties
    D. trying to do as little work as possible

35. The CHIEF reason for an employee training program is to 35.____
    A. increase the efficiency of the employee's work
    B. train the employee for promotion examinations
    C. to meet and talk with each new employee
    D. to give the supervisor an opportunity to reprimand the employee for his lack of knowledge

36. A supervisor may encourage his subordinates to make suggestions by 36.____
    A. keeping a record of the number of suggestions an employee makes
    B. providing a suggestion box
    C. outlining a list of possible suggestions
    D. giving credit to a subordinate whose suggestion has been accepted and used

37. The statement that accuracy is of greater importation than speed means MOST NEARLY that 37.____
    A. slower work increases employment
    B. fast workers may be inferior workers
    C. there are many varieties of work to do in an office
    D. the slow worker is the most efficient person

38. To print tabular material is always much more expensive than to print straight text. 38.____
It follows MOST NEARLY that
   A. the more columns and subdivisions there are in a table, the more expensive is the printing
   B. the omission of the number and title from a table reduces printing costs
   C. it is always desirable to only print straight text
   D. do not print tabular material as it is too expensive

39. If you were required to give service ratings to employees under your supervision, you should consider as MOST important, during the current period, the 39.____
   A. personal characteristics and salary and grade of an employee
   B. length of service and the volume of work performed
   C. previous service rating given him
   D. personal characteristics and the quality of work of an employee

40. If a representative committee of employees in a large department is to meet with an administrative officer for the purpose of improving staff relations and of handling grievances, it is BEST that these meetings be held 40.____
   A. at regular intervals
   B. whenever requested b an aggrieved employee
   C. whenever the need arises
   D. at the discretion of the administrative officer

41. In order to be best able to teach a newly appointed employee who must learn to do a type of work which is unfamiliar to him, his supervisor should realize that during this first stage in the learning process the subordinate is GENERALLY characterized by 41.____
   A. acute consciousness of self
   B. acute consciousness of subject matter, with little interest in persons or personalities
   C. inertness or passive acceptance of assigned role
   D. understanding of problems without understanding of the means of solving them

42. The MOST accurate of the following principles of education and learning for a supervisor to keep in mind when planning a training program for the assistant supervisors under her supervision is that 42.____
   A. assistant supervisors, like all other individuals, vary in the rate at which they learn new material and in the degree to which they can retain what they do learn
   B. experienced assistant supervisors who have the same basic college education and agency experience will be able to learn new material at approximately the same rate of speed
   C. the speed with which assistant supervisors can learn new material after the age of forty is half as rapid as at ages twenty to thirty
   D. with regard to any specific task, it is easier and takes less time to break an experienced assistant supervisor of old, unsatisfactory work habits than it is to teach him new, acceptable ones

43. A supervisor has been transferred from supervision of one group of units to another group of units in the same center. She spends the first three weeks in her new assignment in getting acquainted with her new subordinates, their caseload problems and their work. In this process, she notices that some of the cash records and forms which are submitted to her by two of the assistant supervisors are carelessly or improperly prepared. 43.____
The BEST of the following actions for the supervisor to take in this situation is to
   A. carefully check the work submitted by these assistant supervisors during an additional three weeks before taking any more positive action
   B. confer with these offending workers and show each one where her work needs improvement and how to go about achieving it
   C. institute an in-service training program specifically designed to solve such a problem and instruct the entire subordinate staff in proper work methods
   D. make a note of these errors for documentary use in preparing the annual service rating reports and advise the workers involved to prepare their work more carefully

44. A supervisor, who was promoted to this position a year ago, has supervised a certain assistant supervisor for this one year. The work of the assistant supervisor has been very poor because he has done a minimum of work, refused to take sufficient responsibility, been difficult to handle, and required very close supervision. Apparently due to the increasing insistence by his supervisor that he improve the caliber of his work, the assistant supervisor tenders his resignation, stating that the demands of the job are too much for him. The opinion of the previous supervisor, who had supervised this assistant supervisor for two years, agrees substantially with that of the new supervisor. 44.____
Under such circumstances, the BEST of the following actions the supervisor can take, in general, is to
   A. recommend that the resignation be accepted and that he be rehired should he later apply when he feels able to do the job
   B. recommend that the resignation be accepted and that he not be rehired should he later so apply
   C. refuse to accept the resignation but try to persuade the assistant supervisor to accept psychiatric help
   D. refuse to accept the resignation, promising the assistant supervisor that he will be less closely supervised in the future since he is now so experienced

45. Rumors have arisen to the effect that one of the staff investigators under your supervision has been attending classes at a local university during afternoon hours when he is supposed to be making field visits. 45.____
The BEST of the following ways for you to approach this problem is to
   A. disregard the rumors since, like most rumors, they probably have no actual foundation in fact
   B. have a discreet investigation made in order to determine the actual facts prior to taking any other action

C. inform the investigator that you know what he has been doing and that such behavior is overt dereliction of duty and is punishable by dismissal
D. review the investigator's work record, spot check his cases, and take no further action unless the quality of his work is below average for the unit

46. A supervisor must consider many factors in evaluating a worker whom he has supervised for a considerable time. 46.____
In evaluating the capacity of such a worker to use independent judgment, the one of the following to which the supervisor should generally give MOST consideration is the worker's
A. capacity to establish good relationships with people (clients, colleagues)
B. educational background
C. emotional stability
D. the quality and judgment shown by the worker in previous work situations known to the supervisor

47. A supervisor is conducting a special meeting with the assistant supervisors under her supervision to read and discuss some major complex changes in the rules and procedures. She notices that one of the assistant supervisors who is normally attentive at meetings seems to be paying no attention to what is being said. The supervisor stops reading the rules and asks the assistant supervisor a couple of questions about the changed procedure, to which she gets satisfactory answers. 47.____
The BEST action of the following for the supervisor to take at the meeting is to
A. advise the assistant supervisor gently but firmly that these changes are complex and that her undivided attention is required in order to fully comprehend them
B. avoid further embarrassment to the assistant supervisor by asking the group as a whole to pay more attention to what is being read
C. discontinue the questioning and resume reading the procedure
D. politely request the assistant supervisor to stop giving those present the impression that she is uninterested in what goes on about her

48. A supervisor becomes aware that one of her very competent experienced workers never takes notes during an interview with a client except to note an occasional name, address, or date. When asked about this practice by the supervisor, the worker states that she has a good memory for important details and has always been able to satisfactorily record an interview after the client has left. 48.____
It would generally be BEST for the supervisor to handle this situation by
A. discussing with her that more extensive note-taking may sometimes be desirable with a client who believes note-taking to be evidence that his problem will receive serious consideration
B. agreeing with this practice since note-taking interferes with the establishment of a proper worker-client relationship
C. explaining that, since interviewing is an art form rather than an exact science, a good worker must devise her own personal rules for interviewing and not be bound by general principles

D. warning the worker that memory is too uncertain a thing to be relied upon and, therefore, notes should be taken during an interview of all matters

49. When an experienced subordinate who has the authority and information necessary to make a decision on a certain difficult matter brings the matter to his supervisor without having made the decision, it would generally be BEST for the supervisor to 49.____
   A. agree to make the decision for the subordinate after the subordinate has explained why he finds it difficult to make the decision and after he has made a recommendation
   B. make the decision for the subordinate, explaining to him the reasons for arriving at the decision
   C. refuse to make the decision, but discuss the various alternatives with the subordinate in order to clarify the issues involved
   D. refuse to make the decision, explaining to the subordinate that he is deemed to be fully qualified and competent to make the decision

50. The one of the following instances when it is MOST important for an upper level supervisor to follow the chain of command is when he is 50.____
   A. communicating decisions
   B. communicating information
   C. receiving suggestions
   D. seeking information

KEY (CORRECT ANSWERS)

1.	C	11.	D	21.	C	31.	A	41.	A
2.	D	12.	B	22.	B	32.	B	42.	A
3.	D	13.	B	23.	B	33.	C	43.	B
4.	A	14.	C	24.	B	34.	C	44.	B
5.	D	15.	D	25.	D	35.	A	45.	B
6.	A	16.	B	26.	D	36.	D	46.	D
7.	D	17.	C	27.	D	37.	B	47.	C
8.	C	18.	D	28.	C	38.	A	48.	A
9.	D	19.	B	29.	B	39.	D	49.	C
10.	B	20.	D	30.	D	40.	A	50.	A

TEST 3

DIRECTIONS: Each question or incomplete statement is followed by several suggested answers or completions. Select the one that BEST answers the question or completes the statement. *PRINT THE LETTER OF THE CORRECT ANSWER IN THE SPACE AT THE RIGHT.*

1. Experts in the field of personnel relations feel that it is generally bad practice for subordinate employees to become aware of pending or contemplated changes in policy or organizational set-up via the "grapevine" CHIEFLY because 1.____
   A. evidence that one or more responsible officials have proved untrustworthy will undermine confidence in the agency
   B. the information disseminated by this method is seldom entirely accurate and generally spreads needless unrest among the subordinate staff
   C. the subordinate staff may conclude that the administration feels the staff cannot be trusted with the true information
   D. the subordinate staff may conclude that the administration lacks the courage to make an unpopular announcement through officials channels

2. In order to maintain a proper relationship with a worker who is assigned to staff rather than line functions, a line supervisor should 2.____
   A. accept all recommendations of the staff worker
   B. include the staff worker in the conferences called by the supervisor for his subordinates
   C. keep the staff worker informed of developments in the area of his staff assignment
   D. require that the staff worker's recommendations be communicated to the supervisor through the supervisor's own superior

3. Of the following, the GREATEST disadvantage of placing a worker in a staff position under the direct supervision of the supervisor whom he advises is the possibility that the 3.____
   A. staff worker will tend to be insubordinate because of a feeling of superiority over the supervisor
   B. staff worker will tend to give advice of the type which the supervisor wants to hear or finds acceptable
   C. supervisor will tend to be mistrustful of the advice of a worker of subordinate rank
   D. supervisor will tend to derive little benefit from the advice because to supervise properly he should know at least as much as his subordinate

4. One factor which might be given consideration in deciding upon the optimum span of control of a supervisor over his immediate subordinates is the position of the supervisor in the hierarchy of the organization. It is generally considered proper that the number of subordinates immediately supervised by a higher, upper echelon, supervisor 4.____
   A. is unrelated to and tends to form no pattern with the number supervised by lower level supervisors
   B. should be about the same as the number supervised by a lower level supervisor

C. should be larger than the number supervised by a lower level supervisor
D. should be smaller than the number supervised by a lower level supervisor

5. An important administrative problem is how precisely to define the limits on authority that is delegated to subordinate supervisors. 5.____
Such definition of limits of authority should be
A. as precise as possible and practicable in all areas
B. as precise as possible and practicable in areas of function, but should allow considerable flexibility in the area of personnel management
C. as precise as possible and practicable in the area of personnel management, but should allow considerable flexibility in the areas of function
D. in general terms so as to allow considerable flexibility both in the areas of function and in the areas of personnel management

6. The LEAST important of the following reasons why a particular activity should be assigned to a unit which performs activities dissimilar to it is that 6.____
A. close coordination is needed between the particular activity and other activities performed by the unit
B. it will enhance the reputation and prestige of the unit supervisor
C. the unit makes frequent use of the results of this particular activity
D. the unit supervisor has a sound knowledge and understanding of the particular activity

7. A supervisor is put in charge of a special unit. She is exceptionally well-qualified for this assignment by her training and experience. One of her very close personal friends has been working for some time as a field investigator in this unit. Both the supervisor and investigator are certain that the rest of the investigators in the unit, many of whom have been in the bureau for a long time, know of this close relationship. 7.____
Under these circumstances, the MOST advisable action for the supervisor to take is to
A. ask that either she be allowed to return to her old assignment, or, if that cannot be arranged, that her friend be transferred to another unit in the center
B. avoid any overt sign of favoritism by acting impartially and with greater reserve when dealing with this investigator than the rest of the staff
C. discontinue any socializing with this investigator either inside or outside the office so as to eliminate any gossip or dissatisfaction
D. talk the situation over with the other investigators and arrive at a mutually acceptable plan of proper office decorum

8. The one of the following causes of clerical error which is usually considered to be LEAST attributable to faulty supervision or inefficient management is 8.____
A. inability to carry out instructions
B. too much work to do
C. an inappropriate record-keeping system
D. continual interruptions

9. Assume that you are the supervisor of a clerical unit in a government agency. One of your subordinates violates a rule of the agency, a violation which requires that the employee be suspended from his work for one day. The violated rule is one that you have found to be unduly strict and you have recommended to the management of the agency that the rule be changed or abolished. The management has been considering your recommendation but has not yet reached a decision on the matter. 9.____
In these circumstances, you should
   A. not initiate disciplinary action, but, instead explain to the employee that the rule may be changed shortly
   B. delay disciplinary action on the violation until the management has reached a decision on changing the rule
   C. modify the disciplinary action by reprimanding the employee and informing him that further action may be taken when the management has reached a decision on changing the rule
   D. initiate the prescribed disciplinary action without commenting on the strictness of the rule or on your recommendation

10. Assume that a supervisor praises his subordinates for satisfactory aspects of their work only when he is about to criticize them for unsatisfactory aspects of their work. 10.____
Such a practice is undesirable PRIMARILY because
   A. his subordinates may expect to be praised for their work even if it is unsatisfactory
   B. praising his subordinates for some aspects of their work while criticizing other aspects will weaken the effects of the criticisms
   C. his subordinates would be more receptive to criticism if it were followed by praise
   D. his subordinates may come to disregard praise and wait for criticism to be given

11. The one of the following which would be the BEST reason for an agency to eliminate a procedure for obtaining and recording certain information is that 11.____
   A. it is no longer legally required to obtain the information
   B. there is an advantage in obtaining the information
   C. the information could be compiled on the basis of other information available
   D. the information obtained is sometimes incorrect

12. In determining the type and number of records to be kept in an agency, it is important to recognize that records are of value PRIMARILY as 12.____
   A. raw material to be used in statistical analysis
   B. sources of information about the agency's activities
   C. by-products of the activities carried on by the agency
   D. data for evaluating the effectiveness of the agency

Questions 13-17.

DIRECTIONS: Each of Questions 13 through 17 consists of a statement which contains one word that is incorrectly used because it is not in keeping with the meaning that the statement is evidently intended to convey. For each of these questions, you are to select the incorrectly used word and substitute for it one of the words lettered A, B, C, or D, which helps BEST to convey the meaning of the statement.

13. There has developed in recent years an increasing awareness of the need to measure the quality of management in all enterprises and to seek the principles that can serve as a basis for this improvement. 13.____
   A. growth B. raise C. efficiency D. define

14. It is hardly an exaggeration to deny that the permanence, productivity, and humanity of any industrial system depend upon its ability to utilize the positive and constructive impulses of all who work and upon its ability to arouse and continue interest in the necessary activities. 14.____
   A. develop B. efficiency C. state D. inspiration

15. The selection of managers on the basis of technical knowledge alone seems to recognize that the essential characteristic of management is getting things done through others, thereby demanding skills that are essential in coordinating the activities of subordinates. 15.____
   A. training B. fails
   C. organization D. improving

16. Only when it is deliberate and when it is clearly understood what impressions the ease of communication will probably create in the minds of employees and subordinate management, should top management refrain from commenting on a subject that is of general concern. 16.____
   A. obvious B. benefit C. doubt D. absence

17. Scientific planning of work requires careful analysis of facts and a precise plan of action for the whims and fancies of executives that often provide only a vague indication of work to be done. 17.____
   A. substitutes B. development
   C. preliminary D. comprehensive

18. Assume that you are a supervisor. One of the workers under your supervision is careless about the routine aspects of his work. 18.____
   Of the following, the action MOST likely to develop in this worker a better attitude toward job routines is to demonstrate that
   A. it is just as easy to do his job the right way
   B. organization of his job will leave more time for field work
   C. the routine part of the job is essential to performing a good piece of work
   D. job routines are a responsibility of the worker

19. A supervisor can MOST effectively secure necessary improvement in a worker's office work by 19.____
    A. encouraging the worker to keep abreast of his work
    B. relating the routine part of his job to the total job to be done
    C. helping the worker to establish a good system for covering his office work and holding him to it
    D. informing the worker that he will be required to organize his work more efficiently

20. A supervisor should offer criticism in such a manner that the criticisms is helpful and not overwhelming. 20.____
    Of the following, the LEAST valid inference that can be drawn on the basis of the above statement is that a supervisor should
    A. demonstrate that the criticism is partial and not total
    B. give criticism in such a way that it does not undermine the worker's self-confidence
    C. keep his relationships with the worker objective
    D. keep criticism directed towards general work performance

21. The one of the following areas in which a worker may LEAST reasonably expect direct assistance from the supervisor is in 21.____
    A. building up rapport with all clients
    B. gaining insight into the unmet needs of clients
    C. developing an understanding of community resources
    D. interpreting agency policies and procedures

22. You are informed that a worker under your supervision has submitted a letter complaining of unfair service rating. 22.____
    Of the following, the MOST valid assumption for you to make concerning this worker is that he should be
    A. more adequately supervised in the future
    B. called in for a supervisory conference
    C. given a transfer to some other unit where he may be more happy
    D. given no more consideration than any other inefficient worker

23. Assume that you are a supervisor. You find that a somewhat bewildered worker, newly appointed to the department, hesitates to ask questions for fear of showing his ignorance and jeopardizing his position. 23.____
    Of the following, the BEST procedure for you to follow is to
    A. try to discover the reason for his evident fear of authority
    B. tell him that when he is in doubt about a procedure or a policy he should consult his fellow workers
    C. develop with the worker a plan for more frequent supervisory conferences
    D. explain why each staff member is eager to give him available information that will help him do a good job

24. Of the following, the MOST effective method of helping a newly-appointed employee adjust to his new job is to 24.____
    A. assure him that with experience his uncertain attitudes will be replaced by a professional approach
    B. help him, by accepting him as he is, to have confidence in his ability to handle the job
    C. help him to be on guard against the development of punitive attitudes
    D. help him to recognize the mutability of the agency's policies and procedures

25. Suppose that, as a supervisor, you have scheduled an individual conference with an experienced employee under your supervision. 25.____
    Of the following, the BEST plan of action for this conference is to
    A. discuss the work that the employee is most interested in
    B. plan with the employee to cover any problems that are difficult for him
    C. advise the employee that the conference is his to do with as he sees fit
    D. spot check the employee's work in advance and select those areas for discussion in which the employee has done poor work

26. Of the following, the CHIEF function of a supervisor should be to 26.____
    A. assist in the planning of new policies and the evaluation of existing ones
    B. promote congenial relationships among members of the staff
    C. achieve optimum functioning of each unit and each worker
    D. promote the smooth functioning of job routines

27. The competent supervisor must realize the importance of planning. 27.____
    Of the following, the aspect of planning which is LEAST appropriately considered a responsibility of the supervisor is
    A. long-range planning for the proper functioning of his unit
    B. planning to take care of peak and slack periods
    C. planning to cover agency policies in group conferences
    D. long-range planning to develop community resources

28. The one of the following objectives which should be of LEAST concern to the supervisor in the performance of his duties is to 28.____
    A. help the worker to make friends with all of his fellow employees
    B. be impartial and fair to all members of the staff
    C. stimulate the worker's growth on the job
    D. meet the needs of the individual employee

29. The one of the following which is LEAST properly considered a direct responsibility of the supervisor is 29.____
    A. liaison between the staff and the administrator
    B. interpreting administrative orders and procedures to the employees
    C. training new employees
    D. maintaining staff morale at a high level

30. In order to teach the employee to develop an objective approach, the BEST action for the supervisor to take is to help the worker to 30.____
    A. develop a sincere interest in his job
    B. understand the varied responsibilities that are an integral part of his job
    C. differentiate clearly between himself as a friend and as an employee
    D. find satisfaction in his work

31. If the employee shows excessive submission which indicates a need for dependence on the supervisor in handling an assignment, it would be MOST advisable for the supervisor to 31.____
    A. indicate firmly that the employee-supervisor relationship does not call for submission
    B. define areas of responsibility of employee and supervisor
    C. recognize the employee's need and of supervisor
    D. recognize the employee's need to be sustained and supported and help him by making decisions for him

32. Assume that, as a supervisor, you are conducting a group conference. Of the following, the BEST procedure for you to follow in order to stimulate group discussion is to 32.____
    A. permit the active participation of all members
    B. direct the discussion to an acceptable conclusion
    C. resolve conflicts of opinion among members of the group
    D. present a question for discussion on which the group members have some knowledge or experience

33. Suppose that, as a new supervisor, you wish to inform the staff under your supervision of your methods of operation. Of the following, the BEST procedure for you to follow is to 33.____
    A. advise the staff that they will learn gradually from experience
    B. inform each employee in an individual conference
    C. call a group conference for this purpose
    D. distribute a written memorandum among all members of the staff

34. The MOST constructive and effective method of correcting an employee who has made a mistake is, in general, to 34.____
    A. explain that his evaluation is related to his errors
    B. point out immediately where he erred and tell him how it should have been done
    C. show him how to readjust his methods so as to avoid similar errors in the future
    D. try to discover by an indirect method why the error was made

35. The MOST effective method for the supervisor to follow in order to obtain the cooperation of an employee under his supervision is, wherever possible, to 35.____
    A. maintain a careful record of performance in order to keep the employee on his toes
    B. give the employee recognition in order to promote greater effort and give him more satisfaction in his work

C. try to gain the employee's cooperation for the good of the service
D. advise the employee that his advancement on the job depends on his cooperation

36. Of the following, the MOST appropriate initial course for an employee to take when he is unable to clarify a policy with his supervisor is to 36.____
A. bring up the problem at the next group conference
B. discuss the policy immediately with his fellow employees
C. accept the supervisor's interpretation as final
D. determine what responsibility he has for putting the policy into effect

37. Good administration allows for different treatment of different workers. 37.____
Of the following, the CHIEF implication of this statement is that
A. it would be unfair for the supervisor not to treat all staff members alike
B. fear of favoritism tends to undermine staff morale
C. best results are obtained by individualization within the limits of fair treatment
D. difficult problems call for a different kind of approach

38. The MOST effective and appropriate method of building efficiency and morale in a group of employees is, in general, 38.____
A. by stressing the economic motive
B. through use of the authority inherent in the position
C. by a friendly approach to all
D. by a discipline that is fair but strict

39. Of the following, the LEAST valid basis for the assignment of work to an employee is the 39.____
A. kind of service to be rendered
B. experience and training of the employee
C. health and capacity of the employee
D. racial composition of the community where the office is located

40. The CHIEF justification for staff education, consisting of in-service training, lies in its contribution to 40.____
A. improvement in the quality of work performed
B. recruitment of a better type of employee
C. employee morale, accruing from a feeling of growth on the job
D. the satisfaction that the employee gets on his job

41. Suppose that you are a supervisor. An employee no longer with your department requests you, as his former supervisor, to write a letter recommending him for a position with a private organization. 41.____
Of the following the BEST procedure for you to follow is to include in the letter only information that
A. will help the applicant get the job
B. is clear, factual, and substantiated
C. is known to you personally
D. can readily be corroborated by personal interview

42. Of the following, the MOST important item on which to base the efficiency evaluation of an employee under your supervision is 32.____
    A. the nature of the relationship that he has built up with his fellow employees
    B. how he gets along with his supervisors
    C. his personal habits and skills
    D. the effectiveness of his control over his work

43. According to generally accepted personnel practice, the MOST effective method of building morale in a new employee is to 43.____
    A. exercise caution in praising the employee, lest he become overconfident
    B. give sincere and frank recommendation whenever possible in order to stimulate interest and effort
    C. praise the employee highly even for mediocre performance so that he will be stimulated to do better
    D. warn the employee frequently that he cannot hope to succeed unless he puts forth his best efforts

44. Errors made by newly-appointed employees often follow a predictable pattern. The one of the following errors likely to have LEAST serious consequences is the tendency of a new employee to 44.____
    A. discuss problems that are outside his province with the client
    B. persuade the client to accept the worker's solution of a problem
    C. be two strict in carrying out departmental policy and procedure
    D. depend upon the use of authority due to his inexperience and lack of skill in working with people

45. The MOST effective way for a supervisor to break down a worker's defensive stand against supervisory guidance is to 45.____
    A. come to an understanding with him on the mutual responsibilities involved in the job of the employee and that of the supervisor
    B. tell him he must feel free to express his opinions and to discuss basic problems
    C. show him how to develop toward greater objectivity, sensitivity, and understanding
    D. advise him that it is necessary to carry out agency policy and procedures in order to do a good job

46. Of the following, the LEAST essential function of the supervisor who is conducting a group conference should be to 46.____
    A. keep attention focused on the purpose of the conference
    B. encourage discussion of controversial points
    C. make certain that all possible viewpoints are discussed
    D. be thoroughly prepared in advance

47. When conducting a group conference, the supervisor should be LEAST concerned with 47.____
    A. providing an opportunity for the free interchange of ideas
    B. imparting knowledge and understanding of the work

C. leading the discussion toward a planned goal
D. pointing out where individual workers have erred in work practice

48. If the participants in a group conference are unable to agree on the proper application of a concept to the work of a department, the MOST suitable temporary procedure for the supervisor to follow is to 48.____
A. suggest that each member think the subject through before the next meeting
B. tell the group to examine their differences for possible conflicts with present policies
C. suggest that practices can be changed because of new conditions
D. state the acceptable practice in the agency and whether deviations from such practice can be permitted

49. If an employee is to participate constructively in any group discussion, it is MOST important that he have 49.____
A. advance notice of the agenda for the meeting
B. long experience in the department
C. knowledge and experience in the particular work
D. the ability to assume a leadership role

50. Of the following, the MOST important principle for the supervisor to follow when conducting a group discussion is that he should 50.____
A. move the discussion toward acceptance by the group of a particular point of view
B. express his ideas clearly and succinctly
C. lead the group to accept the authority inherent in his position
D. contribute to the discussion from his knowledge and experience

KEY (CORRECT ANSWERS)

1.	B	11.	C	21.	A	31.	B	41.	B
2.	C	12.	B	22.	B	32.	D	42.	D
3.	B	13.	B	23.	C	33.	C	43.	B
4.	D	14.	C	24.	B	34.	C	44.	C
5.	A	15.	B	25.	B	35.	B	45.	A
6.	B	16.	D	26.	C	36.	D	46.	B
7.	A	17.	A	27.	D	37.	C	47.	D
8.	A	18.	D	28.	A	38.	D	48.	D
9.	D	19.	B	29.	A	39.	D	49.	A
10.	D	20.	D	30.	C	40.	A	50.	D

EXAMINATION SECTION

TEST 1

DIRECTIONS: Each question or incomplete statement is followed by several suggested answers or completions. Select the one that BEST answers the question or completes the statement. *PRINT THE LETTER OF THE CORRECT ANSWER IN THE SPACE AT THE RIGHT.*

1. A supervisor notices that one of his more competent subordinates has recently been showing less interest in his work. The work performed by this employee has also fallen off and he seems to want to do no more than the minimum acceptable amount of work. When his supervisor questions the subordinate about his decreased interest and his mediocre work performance, the subordinate replies: *Sure, I've lost interest in my work. I don' see any reason why I should do more than I have to. When I do a good job, nobody notices it. But, let me fall down on one minor job and the whole place knows about it! So why should I put myself out on this job?* 1.____
   If the subordinate's contentions are true, it would be correct to assume that the
   - A. subordinate has not received adequate training
   - B. subordinate's workload should be decreased
   - C. supervisor must share responsibility for this employee's reaction
   - D. supervisor has not been properly enforcing work standards

2. How many subordinates should report directly to each supervisor? While there is agreement that there are limits to the number of subordinates that a manager can supervise well, this limit is determined by a number of important factors. Which of the following factors is MOST likely to increase the number of subordinates that can be effectively supervised by one supervisor in a particular unit? 2.____
   - A. The unit has a great variety of activities.
   - B. A staff assistant handles the supervisor's routine duties.
   - C. The unit has a relatively inexperienced staff.
   - D. The office layout is being rearranged to make room for more employees.

3. Mary Smith, an Administrative Assistant, heads the Inspection Records Unit of Department Y. She is a dedicated supervisor who not only strives to maintain an efficient operation, but she also tries to improve the competence of each individual member of her staff. She keeps these considerations in mind when assigning work to her staff. Her bureau chief asks her to compile some data based on information contained in her records. She feels that any member of her staff should be able to do this job. 3.____
   The one of the following members of her staff who would probably be given LEAST consideration for this assignment is
   - A. Jane Abel, a capable Supervising Clerk with considerable experience in the unit
   - B. Kenneth Brown, a Senior Clerk recently transferred to the unit who has not had an opportunity to demonstrate his capabilities

C. Laura Chance, a Clerk who spends full time on a single routine assignment
D. Michael Dunn, a Clerk who works on several minor jobs but still has the lightest workload

4. There are very few aspects of a supervisor's job that do not involve communication, either in writing or orally. 4.____
Which of the following statements regarding oral and written orders is NOT correct?
A. Oral orders usually permit more immediate feedback than do written orders.
B. Written orders, rather than oral orders, should generally be given when the subordinate will be held strictly accountable.
C. Oral orders are usually preferable when the order contains lengthy detailed instructions.
D. Written orders, rather than oral orders, should usually be given to a subordinate who is slow to understand or is forgetful.

5. Assume that you are the head of a large clerical unit in Department R. Your department's personnel office has appointed a Clerk, Roberta Rowe, to fill a vacancy in your unit. Before bringing this appointee to your office, the personnel office has given Roberta the standard orientation on salary, fringe benefits, working conditions, attendance, and the department's personnel rules. In addition, he has supplied her with literature covering these areas. 5.____
Of the following, the action that you should take FIRST after Roberta has been brought to your office is to
A. give her an opportunity to read the literature furnished by the personnel office so that she can ask you questions about it
B. escort her to the desk she will use and assign her to work with an experienced employee who will act as her trainer
C. explain the duties and responsibilities of her job and its relationship with the jobs being performed by the other employees of the unit
D. summon the employee who is currently doing the work that will be performed by Roberta and have him explain and demonstrate how to perform the required tasks

6. Your superior informs you that the employee turnover rate in your office is well above the norm and must be reduced. 6.____
Which one of the following initial steps would be LEAST appropriate in attempting to overcome this problem?
A. Decide to be more lenient about performance standards and about employee requests for time off, so that your office will gain a reputation as an easy place to work
B. Discuss the problem with a few of your key people whose judgment you trust to see if they can shed some light on the underlying causes of the problem

C. Review the records of employees who have left during the past year to see if there is a pattern that will help you understand the problem
D. Carefully review your training procedures to see whether they can be improved

7. In issuing instructions to a subordinate on a job assignment, the supervisor should ordinarily explain why the assignment is being made. 7.____
Omission of such an explanation is BEST justified when the
A. subordinate is restricted in the amount of discretion he can exercise in carrying out the assignment
B. assignment is one that will be unpopular with the subordinate
C. subordinate understands the reason as a result of previous similar assignments
D. assignment is given to an employee who is in need of further training

8. When a supervisor allows sufficient time for training and makes an appropriate effort in the training of his subordinates, his CHIEF goal is to 8.____
A. increase the dependence of one subordinate upon another in their everyday work activities
B. spend more time with his subordinates in order to become more involved in their work
C. increase the capability and independence of his subordinates in carrying out their work
D. increase his frequency of contact with his subordinates in order to better evaluate their performance

9. In preparing an evaluation of a subordinate's performance, which one of the following items is usually irrelevant? 9.____
A. Remarks about tardiness or absenteeism
B. Mention of any unusual contributions or accomplishments
C. A summary of the employee's previous job experience
D. An assessment of the employee's attitude toward the job

10. The ability to delegate responsibility while maintaining adequate controls is one key to a supervisor's success. 10.____
Which one of the following methods of control would minimize the amount of responsibility assumed by the subordinate?
A. Asking for a monthly status report in writing
B. Asking to receive copies of important correspondence so that you can be aware of potential problems
C. Scheduling periodic project status conferences with your subordinate
D. Requiring that your subordinate confer with you before making decisions on a project

11. You wish to assign an important project to a subordinate who you think has good potential. 11.____
Which one of the following approaches would be MOST effective in successfully completing the project while developing the subordinate's abilities?
A. Describe the project to the subordinate in general terms and emphasize that it must be completed as quickly as possible
B. Outline the project in detail to the subordinate and emphasize that its successful completion could lead to career advancement
C. Develop a detailed project outline and timetable, discuss the details and timing with him and assign the subordinate to carry out the plan on his own
D. Discuss the project objectives and suggested approaches with the subordinate, and ask the subordinate to develop a detailed project outline and timetable of your approval

12. Research studies reveal that an important difference between high-production and low-production supervisors lies not in their interest in eliminating mistakes, but in their manner of handling mistakes. 12.____
High-production supervisors are MOST likely to look upon mistakes as primarily
A. an opportunity to provide training
B. a byproduct of subordinate negligence
C. an opportunity to fix blame in a situation
D. a result of their own incompetence

13. Supervisors should try to establish what has been called *positive discipline*, an atmosphere in which subordinates willingly abide by rules which they consider fair. 13.____
When a supervisor notices a subordinate violating an important rule, his FIRST course of action should be to
A. stop the subordinate and tell him what he is doing wrong
B. wait a day or two before approaching the employee involved
C. call a meeting of all subordinates to discuss the rule
D. forget the matter in the hope that it will not happen again

14. The working climate is the feeling, degree of freedom, the tone and the mood of the working environment. 14.____
Which of the following contributes MOST to determining the working climate in a unit or group?
A. The rules set for rest periods
B. The example set by the supervisor
C. The rules set for morning check-in
D. The wages paid to the employee

15. John Polk is a bright, ingenious clerk with a lot of initiative. He has made many good suggestions to his supervisor in the Training Division of Department T, where he is employed. However, last week one of his bright ideas literally *blew up*. In setting up some electronic equipment in the training classroom, he cross some wires resulting in a damaged tape recorder and a classroom so filled with smoke that the training class had to be held in another room. When Mr. Brown, his supervisor, learned of this occurrence, he immediately summoned John to his private office. There Mr. Brown spent five minutes bawling John out, calling him an overzealous, overgrown kid, and send him back to his job without letting John speak once. 15.____
Of the following, the action of Mr. Brown that MOST deserves approval is that he
   A. took disciplinary action immediately without regard for past performance
   B. kept the disciplinary interview to a brief period
   C. concentrated his criticism on the root cause of the occurrence
   D. held the disciplinary interview in his private office

16. Typically, when the technique of *supervision by results* is practiced, higher management sets down, either implicitly or explicitly, certain performance standards or goals that the subordinate is expected to meet. So long as these standards are met, management interferes very little. 16.____
The MOST likely result of the use of this technique is that it will
   A. lead to ambiguity in terms of goals
   B. be successful only to the extent that close direct supervision is practiced
   C. make it possible to evaluate both employee and supervisory effectiveness
   D. allow for complete autonomy on the subordinate's part

17. Assume that you, an Administrative Assistant, are the supervisor of a large clerical unit performing routine clerical operations. One of your clerks consistently produces much less work than other members of our staff performing similar tasks. 17.____
Of the following, the action you should take FIRST is to
   A. ask the clerk if he wants to be transferred to another unit
   B. reprimand the clerk for his poor performance and warn him that further disciplinary action will be taken if his work does not improve
   C. quietly ask the clerk's co-workers whether they know why his performance is poor
   D. discuss this matter with the clerk to work out plans for improving his performance

18. When making written evaluations and reviews of the performance of subordinates, it is usually ADVISABLE to 18.____
   A. avoid informing the employee of the evaluation if it is critical because it may create hard feelings
   B. avoid informing the employee of the evaluation whether critical or favorable because it is tension-producing

C. permit the employee to see the evaluation but not to discuss it with him because the supervisor cannot be certain where the discussion might lead
D. discuss the evaluation openly with the employee because it helps the employee understand what is expected of him

19. There are a number of well-known and respected human relations principles that successful supervisors have been using for years in building good relationships with their employees. 19.____
Which of the following does NOT illustrate such a principle?
A. Give clear and complete instructions
B. Let each person know how he is getting along
C. Keep an open-door policy
D. Make all relationships personal ones

20. Assume that it is your responsibility as an Administrative Assistant to maintain certain personnel records that are continually being updated. You have three senior clerks assigned specifically to this task. Recently, you have noticed that the volume of work has increased substantially, and the processing of personnel records by the clerks is backlogged. Your supervisor is now receiving complaints due to the processing delay. 20.____
Of the following, the BEST course of action for you to take FIRST is to
A. have a meeting with the clerks, advise them of the problem, and ask that they do their work faster; then confirm your meeting in writing for the record
B. request that an additional position be authorized for your unit
C. review the procedures being used for processing the work, and try to determine if you can improve the flow of work
D. get the system moving faster by spending some of your own time processing the backlog

21. Assume that you are in charge of a payroll unit consisting of four clerks. It is Friday, November 14. You have just arrived in the office after a conference. Your staff is preparing a payroll that must be forwarded the following Monday. 21.____
Which of the following new items on your desk should you attend to FIRST?
A. A telephone message regarding very important information needed for the statistical summary of salaries paid for the month of November
B. A memorandum regarding a new procedure that should be followed in preparing the payroll
C. A telephone message from an employee who is threatening to endorse his paycheck *Under Protest* because he is dissatisfied with the amount
D. A memorandum from your supervisor reminding you to submit the probationary period report on a new employee

22. You are an Administrative Assistant in charge of a unit that orders and issues supplies. On a particular day you are faced with the following four situations. 22.____
Which one should you take care of FIRST?

A. One of your employees who is in the process of taking the quarterly inventory of supplies has telephoned and asked that you return his call as soon as possible
B. A representative of a company that is noted for producing excellent office supplies will soon arrive with samples for you to distribute to the various offices in your agency
C. A large order of supplies which was delivered this morning has been checked and counted and a deliveryman is waiting for you to sign the receipt
D. A clerk from the purchase division asks you to search for a bill you failed to send to them which is urgently needed in order for them to complete a report due this morning

23. As an Administrative Assistant, assume that it is necessary for you to give an unpleasant assignment to one of your subordinates. You expect this employee to raise some objections to this assignment. 23.____
The MOST appropriate of the following actions for you to take FIRST is to issue the assignment
A. orally, with the further statement that you will not listen to any complaints
B. in writing, to forestall any complaints by the employee
C. orally, permitting the employee to express his feelings
D. in writing, with a note that any comments should be submitted in writing

24. Assume that you are an Administrative Assistant supervising the Duplicating and Reproduction Unit of Department B. One of your responsibilities is to prepare a daily schedule showing when and on which of your unit's four duplicating machine jobs are to be run off. 24.____
Of the following, the factor that should be given LEAST consideration in preparing the schedule is the
A. priority of each of the jobs to be run off
B. production speed of the different machines that will be used
C. staff available to operate the machines
D. date on which the job order was received

25. Cycling is an arrangement where papers are processed throughout a period according to an orderly plan rather than as a group all at one time. This technique has been used for a long time by public utilities in their cycle billing. 25.____
Of the following practices, the one that BEST illustrates this technique is that in which
A. paychecks for per annum employees are issued bi-weekly and those for per diem employees are issued weekly
B. field inspectors report in person to their offices one day a week, on Fridays, when they do all their paperwork and also pick up their paychecks
C. the dates for issuing relief checks to clients vary depending on the last digit of the clients' social security numbers
D. the last day for filing and paying income taxes is the same for Federal, State, and City income taxes

26. The employees in your division have recently been given an excellent up-to-date office manual, but you find that a good number of employees are not following the procedures outlined in it. 26.____
Which one of the following would be MOST likely to ensure that employees begin using the manual effectively?
   A. Require each employee to keep a copy of the manual in plain sight on his desk
   B. Issue warnings periodically to those employees who deviate most from procedures prescribed in the manual
   C. Tell an employee to check his manual when he does not follow the proper procedures
   D. Suggest to the employees that the manual be studied thoroughly

27. The one of the following factors which should be considered FIRST in the design of office forms is the 27.____
   A. information to be included in the form
   B. sequence of the information
   C. purpose of the form
   D. persons who will be using the form

28. Window envelopes are being used to an increasing extent by government and private industry. 28.____
The one of the following that is NOT an advantage of window envelopes is that they
   A. cut down on addressing costs
   B. eliminate the need to attach envelopes to letters being sent forward for signature by a superior
   C. are less costly to buy than regular envelopes

29. Your bureau head asks you to prepare the office layouts for several of his units being moved to a higher floor in your office building. 29.____
Of the following possibilities, the one that you should AVOID in preparing the layouts is to
   A. place the desks of the first-line supervisors near those of the staffs they supervise
   B. place the desks of employees whose work is most closely related near one another
   C. arrange the desks so that employees do not face one another
   D. locate desks with many outside visitors farthest from the office entrance

30. Which one of the following conditions would be LEAST important in considering a change of the layout in a particular office? 30.____
   A. Installation of a new office machine
   B. Assignment of five additional employees to your office
   C. Poor flow of work
   D. Employees' personal preferences of desk location

31. Suppose Mr. Bloom, an Administrative Assistant, is dictating a letter to a stenographer. His dictation begins with the name of the addressee and continues to the body of the letter. However, Mr. Bloom does not dictate the address of the recipient of the letter. He expects the stenographer to locate it. The use of this practice by Mr. Bloom is 31.____
   A. *acceptable*, especially if he gives the stenographer the letter to which he is responding
   B. *acceptable*, especially if the letter is lengthy and detailed
   C. *unacceptable*, because it is not part of a stenographer's duties to search for information
   D. *unacceptable*, because he should not rely on the accuracy of the stenographer

32. Assume that there are no rules, directives or instructions concerning the filing of materials in your office or the retention of such files. A system is now being followed of placing in inactive files any materials that are more than one year old. 32.____
Of the following, the MOST appropriate thing to do with material that has been in an inactive file in your office for more than one year is to
   A. inspect the contents of the files to decide how to dispose of them
   B. transfer the material to a remote location, where it can be obtained if necessary
   C. keep the material intact for a minimum of another three years
   D. destroy the material which has not been needed for at least a year

33. Suppose you, an Administrative Assistant, have just returned to your desk after engaging in an all-morning conference. Joe Burns, a Clerk, informs you that Clara McClough, an administrator in another agency, telephoned during the morning and that, although she requested to speak with you, he was able to give her the desired information. 33.____
Of the following, the MOST appropriate action for you to take in regard to Mr. Burns' action is to
   A. thank him for assisting Ms. McClough in your absence
   B. explain to him the proper telephone practice to use in the future
   C. reprimand him for not properly channeling Ms. McClough's call
   D. issue a memo to all clerical employees regarding proper telephone practices

34. When interviewing subordinates with problems, supervisors frequently find that asking direct questions of the employee results only in evasive responses. The supervisor may, therefore, resort to the non-directive interview technique. In this technique, the supervisor avoids pointed questions; he leads the employee to continue talking freely uninfluenced by the supervisor's preconceived notions. This technique often enables the employee to bring his problem into sharp focus and to reach a solution to his problem. Suppose that you are a supervisor interviewing a subordinate about his recent poor attendance record. 34.____

On calling his attention to his excessive lateness record, he replies: *I just don't seem to be able to get up in the morning. Frankly, I've lost interest in this job. don't care about it. When I get up in the morning, I have to skip breakfast and I'm still late. I don't care about this job.*
If you are using the non-directive technique in this interview, the MOST appropriate of the following responses for you to make is
A. You don't care about this job?
B. Don't you think you are letting your department down?
C. Are you having trouble at home?
D. Don't you realize your actions are childish?

35. An employee in a work group made the following comment to a co-worker: *It's great to be a lowly employee instead of an Administrative Assistant because you can work without thinking. The Administrative Assistant is getting paid to plan, schedule, and think. Let him see to it that you have a productive day.* 35.____
Which one of the following statements about his quotation BEST reflects an understanding of good personnel management techniques and the role of the supervising Administrative Assistant?
A. The employee is wrong in attitude and in his perception of the role of the Administrative Assistant.
B. The employee is correct in attitude but is wrong in his perception of the role of the Administrative Assistant.
C. The employee is correct in attitude and in his perception of the role of the Administrative Assistant.
D. The employee is wrong in attitude but is right in his perception of the role of the Administrative Assistant.

KEY (CORRECT ANSWERS)

1.	C	11.	D	21.	B	31.	A
2.	B	12.	A	22.	C	32.	A/B
3.	A	13.	A	23.	C	33.	A
4.	C	14.	B	24.	D	34.	A
5.	C	15.	D	25.	C	35.	D
6.	A	16.	C/D	26.	C		
7.	C	17.	D	27.	C		
8.	C	18.	D	28.	C		
9.	C	19.	D	29.	D		
10.	D	20.	C	30.	D		

TEST 2

DIRECTIONS: Each question or incomplete statement is followed by several suggested answers or completions. Select the one that BEST answers the question or completes the statement. *PRINT THE LETTER OF THE CORRECT ANSWER IN THE SPACE AT THE RIGHT.*

Questions 1-5.

DIRECTIONS: Questions 1 through 5 are to be answered SOLELY on the basis of the following passage.

General supervision, in contrast to close supervision, involves a high degree of delegation of authority and requires some indirect means to ensure that employee behavior conforms to management needs. Not everyone works well under general supervision; however, general supervision works best where subordinates desire responsibility. General supervision also works well where individuals in work groups have strong feelings about the quality of the finished work products. Strong identification with management goals is another trait of persons who work well under general supervision. There are substantial differences in the amount of responsibility people are willing to accept on the job. One person lay flourish under supervision that another might find extremely restrictive.

Psychological research provides evidence that the nature of a person's personality affects his attitude toward supervision. There are some employees with a low need for achievement and high fear of failure who shy away from challenges and responsibilities. Many seek self-expression off the job and ask only to be allowed to daydream on it. There are others who have become so accustomed to the authoritarian approach in their culture, family and previous work experience that they regard general supervision as no supervision at all. They abuse the privileges it bestows on them and refuse to accept the responsibilities it demands.

Different groups develop different attitudes toward work. Most college graduates, for example, expect a great deal of responsibility and freedom. People with limited education, on the other hand, often have trouble accepting the concept that people should make decisions for themselves, particularly decisions concerning work. Therefore, the extent to which general supervision will be effective varies greatly with the subordinates involved.

1. According to the above passage, which one of the following is a NECESSARY part of management policy regarding general supervision? 1.____
   A. Most employees should formulate their own work goals.
   B. Deserving employees should be rewarded periodically.
   C. Some controls on employee work patterns should be established.
   D. Responsibility among employees should generally be equalized.

2. It can be inferred from the above passage that an employee who avoids responsibilities and challenges is MOST likely to 2.____
   A. gain independence under general supervision
   B. work better under close supervision than under general supervision
   C. abuse the liberal guidelines of general supervision
   D. become more restricted and cautious under general supervision

3. Based on the above passage, employees who succeed under general supervision are MOST likely to 3.____
   A. have a strong identification with people and their problems
   B. accept work obligations without fear
   C. seek self-expression off the job
   D. value the intellectual aspects of life

4. Of the following, the BEST title for the passage is 4.____
   A. Benefits and Disadvantages of General Supervision
   B. Production Levels of Employees Under General Supervision
   C. Employee Attitudes Toward Work and the Work Environment
   D. Employee Background and Personality as a Factor in Utilizing General Supervision

5. It can be inferred from the above passage that the one of the following employees who is MOST likely to work best under general supervision is one who 5.____
   A. is a part-time graduate student
   B. was raised by very strict parents
   C. has little confidence
   D. has been closely supervised in past jobs

Questions 6-10.

DIRECTIONS: Questions 6 through 10 are to be answered SOLELY on the basis of the following passage.

The concept of *program management* was first developed in order to handle some of the complex projects undertaken by the U.S. Department of Defense in the 1950's. Program management is an administrative system combining planning and control techniques to guide and coordinate all the activities which contribute to one overall program or project. It has been used by the federal government to manage space exploration and other programs involving many contributing organizations. It is also used by state and local governments and by some large firms to provide administrative integration of work from a number of sources, be they individuals, departments or outside companies.

One of the specific administrative techniques for program management is Program Evaluation Review Technique (PERT). PERT begins with the assembling of a list of all the activities needed to accomplish an overall task. The next step consists of arranging these activities in a sequential network showing both how much time each activity will take and which activities must be completed before others can begin. The time required for each activity is estimated by simple statistical techniques by the persons who will be responsible for the work, and the time required to complete the entire string of activities along each sequential path through the network is then calculated. There may be dozens or hundreds of these paths, so the calculation is usually done by computer. The longest path is then labeled the *critical path* because no matter how quickly events not on this path are completed, the events long the longest path must be finished before the project can be terminated. The overall starting and completion dates are then pinpointed, and target dates are established for each task. Actual progress can later be checked by comparison to the network plan.

6. Judging from the information in the above passage, which one of the following projects is MOST suitable for handling by a program management technique? 6.____
   A. Review and improvement of the filing system used by a city office
   B. Computerization of accounting data already on file in an office
   C. Planning and construction of an urban renewal project
   D. Announcing a change in city tax regulations to thousands of business firms

7. The above passage indicates that program management methods are now in wide use by various kinds of organizations. 7.____
   Which one of the following organizations would you LEAST expect to make much use of such methods today?
   A. An automobile manufacturer
   B. A company in the aerospace business
   C. The government of a large city
   D. A library reference department

8. In making use of the PERT technique, the FIRST step is to determine 8.____
   A. every activity that must take place in order to complete the project
   B. a target date for completion of the project
   C. the estimated time required to complete each activity which is related to the whole
   D. which activities will make up the longest path on the chart

9. Who estimates the time required to complete a particular activity in a PERT program? 9.____
   A. The people responsible for the particular activity
   B. The statistician assigned to the program
   C. The organization that has commissioned the project
   D. The operator who programs the computer

10. Which one of the following titles BEST describes the contents of the passage? 10.____
    A. The Need For Computers in Today's Projects
    B. One Technique For Program Management
    C. Local Governments Can Now Use Space-Age Techniques
    D. Why Planning Is Necessary For Complex Projects

11. An Administrative Assistant has been criticized for the low productivity in the group which he supervises. 11.____
    Which of the following BEST reflects an understanding of supervisory responsibilities in the area of productivity?
    An Administrative Assistant should be held responsible for his own
    A. individual productivity and the productivity of the group he supervises, because he is in a position where he maintains or increases production through others
    B. personal productivity only, because the supervisor is not likely to have any effect on the productivity of subordinates

C. individual productivity but only for a drop in the productivity of the group he supervises, since subordinates will receive credit for increased productivity individually
D. personal productivity only, because this is how he would be evaluated if he were not a supervisor

12. A supervisor has held a meeting in his office with an employee about the employee's grievance. The grievance concerned the sharp way in which the supervisor reprimanded the employee for an error the employee made in the performance of a task assigned to him. The problem was not resolved. Which one of the following statements about this meeting BEST reflects an understanding of good supervisory techniques? 12.____
A. It is awkward for a supervisor to handle a grievance involving himself. The supervisor should not have held the meeting.
B. It would have been better is the supervisor had held the meeting at the employee's workplace, even though there would have been frequent distractions, because the employee would have been more relaxed.
C. The resolution of a problem is not the only sign of a successful meeting. The achievement of communication was worthwhile.
D. The supervisor should have been forceful. There is nothing wrong with raising your voice to an employee every once in a while.

13. John Hayden, the owner of a single-family house, complains that he submitted an application for reduction of assessment that obviously was not acted upon before his final assessment notice was sent to him. The timely receipt of the application has been verified in a departmental log book.
As the supervisor of the clerical unit through which this application was processed and where this delay occurred, you should be LEAST concerned with 13.____
A. what happened
B. who is responsible
C. why it happened
D. what can be learned from it

14. The one of the following that applies MOST appropriate to the role of the first-line supervisor is that usually he is 14.____
A. called upon to help determine agency policy
B. involved in long-range agency planning
C. responsible for determining some aspects of basic organization structure
D. a participant in developing procedures and methods

15. Sally Jones, an Administrative Assistant, gives clear and precise instructions to Robert Warren, a Senior Clerk. In these instructions, Ms. Jones clearly delegates authority to Mr. Warren to undertake a well-defined task.
In this situation, Ms. Jones should expect Mr. Warren to 15.____
A. come to her to check out details as he progresses with the task
B. come to her only with exceptional problems
C. ask her permission if he wishes to use his delegated authority
D. use his authority to redefine the task and its related activities

16. Planning involves establishing departmental goals and programs and determining ways of reaching them. 16.____
The MAIN advantage of such planning is that
A. there will be no need for adjustments once a plan is put into operation
B. it ensures that everyone is working on schedule
C. it provides the framework for an effective operation
D. unexpected work problems are easily overcome

17. As a result of reorganization, the jobs in a large clerical unit were broken down into highly specialized tasks. Each specialized task was then assigned to a particular employee to perform. 17.____
This action will probably lead to an increase in
A. flexibility
B. job satisfaction
C. need for coordination
D. employee initiative

18. Your office carries on a large volume of correspondence concerned with the purchase of supplies and equipment for city offices. You use form letters to deal with many common situations. 18.____
In which one of the following situations would use of a form letter be LEAST appropriate?
A. Informing suppliers of a change in city regulations concerning purchase contracts
B. Telling a new supplier the standard procedures to be followed in billing
C. Acknowledging receipt of a complaint and saying that the complaint will be investigated
D. Answering a city councilman's request for additional information on a particular regulation affecting suppliers

19. Assume that you are an Administrative Assistant heading a large clerical unit. Because of the great demands being made on your time, you have designated Tom Smith, a Supervising Clerk, to be your assistant and to assume some of your duties. 19.____
Of the following duties performed by you, the MOST appropriate one to assign to Tom Smith is to
A. conduct the on-the-job training of new employees
B. prepare the performance appraisal reports on your staff members
C. represent your unit in dealings with the heads of other units
D. handle matters that require exception to general policy

20. In establishing rules for his subordinates, a superior should be PRIMARILY concerned with 20.____
A. creating sufficient flexibility to allow for exceptions
B. making employees aware of the reasons for the rules and the penalties for infractions
C. establishing the strength of his own position in relation to his subordinates
D. having his subordinates know that such rules will be imposed in a personal manner

21. The practice of conducting staff training sessions on a periodic basis is generally considered 21.____
    A. *poor*; it takes employees away from their work assignments
    B. *poor*; all staff training should be done on an individual basis
    C. *good*; it permits the regular introduction of new methods and techniques
    D. *good*; it ensures a high employee productivity rate

22. Suppose, as an Administrative Assistant, you have just announced at a staff meeting with your subordinates that a radical reorganization of work will take place next week. Your subordinates at the meeting appear to be excited, tense, and worried. 22.____
    Of the following, the BEST action for you to take at that time is to
    A. schedule private conferences with each subordinate to obtain his reaction to the meeting
    B. close the meeting and tell your subordinates to return immediately to their work assignments
    C. give your subordinates some time to ask questions and discuss your announcement
    D. insist that your subordinates do not discuss your announcement among themselves or with other members of the agency

23. Suppose that as an Administrative Assistant you were recently placed in charge of the Duplicating and Stock Unit of Department Y. From your observation of the operations of your unit during your first week as its head, you get the impression that there are inefficiencies in its operations causing low productivity. 23.____
    To obtain an increase in its productivity, the FIRST of the following actions you should take is to
    A. seek the advice of your immediate superior on how he would tackle this problem
    B. develop plans to correct any unsatisfactory conditions arising from other than manpower deficiencies
    C. identify the problems causing low productivity
    D. discuss your productivity problem with other unit heads to find out how they handled similar problems

24. Assume that you are an Administrative Assistant recently placed in charge of a large clerical unit. At a meeting, the head of another unit tells you: *My practice is to give a worker more than he can finish. In that way you can be sure that you are getting the most out of him.* 24.____
    For you to accept this practice would be
    A. *advisable*, since your actions would be consistent with those practiced in your agency
    B. *inadvisable*, since such a practice is apt to create frustration and lower staff morals
    C. *advisable* since a high goal stimulates people to strive to attain it
    D. *inadvisable*, since management may, in turn, set too high a productivity goal for the unit

25. Suppose that you are the supervisor of a unit in which there is an increasing amount of friction among several of your staff members. One of the reasons for this friction is that the work of some of these staff members cannot be completed until other staff members complete related work. 25.____
Of the following, the MOST appropriate action for you to take is to
   A. summon these employees to a meeting to discuss the responsibilities each has and to devise better methods of coordination
   B. have a private talk with each employee involved and make each understand that there must be more cooperation among the employees
   C. arrange for interviews with each of the employees involved to determine what his problems are
   D. shift the assignments of these employees so that each will be doing a job different from his current one

26. An office supervisor has a number of responsibilities with regard to his subordinates. 26.____
Which one of the following functions should NOT be regarded as a basic responsibility of the office supervisor?
   A. Telling employees how to solve personal problems that may be interfering with their work
   B. Training new employees to do the work assigned to them
   C. Evaluating employees' performance periodically and discussing the evaluation with each employee
   D. Bringing employee grievances to the attention of higher-level administrators and seeking satisfactory resolutions

27. One of your most productive subordinates frequently demonstrates a poor attitude toward his job. He seems unsure of himself, and he annoys his co-workers because he is continually belittling himself and the work that he is doing. 27.____
In trying to help him overcome this problem, which of the following approaches is LEAST likely to be effective?
   A. Compliment him on his work and assign him some additional responsibilities, telling him that he is being given these responsibilities because of his demonstrated ability
   B. Discuss with him the problem of his attitude, and warn him that you will have to report it on his next performance evaluation
   C. Assign him a particularly important and difficult project, stressing your confidence in his ability to complete it successfully
   D. Discuss with him the problem of his attitude, and ask him for suggestions as to how you can help him overcome it

28. You come to realize that a personality conflict between you and one of your subordinates is adversely affecting his performance. 28.____
Which one of the following would be the MOST appropriate FIRST step to take?
   A. Report the problem to your superior and request assistance. His experience may be helpful in resolving this problem.

B. Discuss the situation with several of the subordinate's co-workers to see if they can suggest any remedy
C. Suggest to the subordinate that he get professional counseling or therapy
D. Discuss the situation candidly with the subordinate, with the objective of resolving the problem between yourselves

29. Assume that you are an Administrative Assistant supervising the Payroll Records Section in Department G. Your section has been requested to prepare and submit to the department's budget officer a detailed report giving a breakdown of labor costs under various departmental programs and sub-programs. You have assigned this task to a Supervising Clerk, giving him full authority for seeing that this job is performed satisfactorily. You have given him a written statement of the job to be done and explained the purpose and use of this report. 29.____
The next step that you should take in connection with this delegated task is to
A. assist the Supervising Clerk in the step-by-step performance of the job
B. assure the Supervising Clerk that you will be understanding of mistakes if made at the beginning
C. require him to receive your approval for interim reports submitted at key points before he can proceed further with his task
D. give him a target date for the completion of this report

30. Assume that you are an Administrative Assistant heading a unit staffed with six clerical employees. One Clerk, John Snell, is a probationary employee appointed four months ago. During the first three months, John learned his job quickly, performed his work accurately and diligently, and was cooperative and enthusiastic in his attitude. However, during the past few weeks his enthusiasm seems dampened, he is beginning to make mistakes and at times appears bored. 30.____
Of the following, the MOST appropriate action for you to take is to
A. check with John's co-workers to find out whether they can explain John's change in attitude and work habits
B. wait a few more weeks before taking any action, so that John will have an opportunity to make the needed changes on his own initiative
C. talk to John about the change in his work performance and his decreased enthusiasm
D. change John's assignment since this may be the basic cause of John's change in attitude and performance

31. The supervisor of a clerical unit, on returning from a meeting, finds that one of his subordinates is performing work not assigned by him. The subordinate explains that the group supervisor had come into the office while the unit supervisor was out and directed the employee to work on an urgent assignment. This is the first time the group supervisor had bypassed the unit supervisor. 31.____
Of the following, the MOST appropriate action for the unit supervisor to take is to

A. explain to the group supervisor that bypassing the unit supervisor is an undesirable practice
B. have the subordinate stop work on the assignment until the entire matter can be clarified with the group supervisor
C. raise the matter of bypassing a supervisor at the next staff conference held by the group supervisor
D. forget about the incident

32. Assume that you are an Administrative Assistant in charge of the Mail and Records Unit of Department K. On returning from a meeting, you notice that Jane Smith is not at her regular work location. You learn that another employee, Ruth Reed, had become faint, and that Jane took Ruth outdoors for some fresh air. It is a long-standing rule in your unit that no employee is to leave the building during office hours except on official business or with the unit head's approval. Only a few weeks ago, John Duncan was reprimanded by you for going out at 10:00 A.M. for a cup of coffee. 32.____
With respect to Jane Smith's violation of this rule, the MOST appropriate of the following actions for you to take is to
A. issue a reprimand to Jane Smith, with an explanation that all employees must be treated in exactly the same way
B. tell Jane that you should reprimand her, but you will not do so in this instance
C. overlook this rule violation in view of the extenuating circumstances
D. issue the reprimand with no further explanation, treating her in the same manner that you treated John Duncan

33. Assume that you are an Administrative Assistant recently assigned as supervisor of Department X's Mail and Special Services Unit. In addition to processing your department's mail, your clerical employees are often sent on errands in the city. You have learned that, while on such official errands, these clerks sometimes take care of their own personal matters or those of their co-workers. The previous supervisor had tolerated this practice even though it violated a departmental personnel rule. 33.____
The MOST appropriate of the following actions for you to take is to
A. continue to tolerate this practice so long as it does not interfere with the work of your unit
B. take no action until you have proof that an employee has violated this rule; then give a mild reprimand
C. wait until an employee has committed a gross violation of this rule; then bring him up on charges
D. discuss this rule with your staff and caution them that its violation might necessitate disciplinary action

34. Supervisor who exercise "close supervision" over their subordinate usually check up on their employees frequently, give them frequent instructions and, in general, limit their freedom to do their work in their own way. Those who exercise "general supervision" usually set forth the objectives of a job, tell their subordinates what they want accomplished, fix the limits within which the subordinates can work and let the employees (if they are capable) decide how the job is to be done. 34.____
Which one of the following conditions would contribute LEAST to the success of the general supervision approach in an organization?
   A. Employees in the unit welcome increased responsibilities
   B. Work assignments in the unit are often challenging
   C. Work procedures must conform with those of other units
   D. Staff members support the objectives of the unit

35. Assume that you are an Administrative Assistant assigned as supervisor of the Clerical Services Unit of a large agency's Labor Relations Division. A member of your staff comes to you with a criticism of a policy followed by the Labor Relations Division. You also have similar views regarding this policy. 35.____
Of the following, the MOST appropriate action for you to take in response to his criticism is to
   A. agree with him, but tell him that nothing can be done about it at your level
   B. suggest to him that it is not wise for him to express criticism of policy
   C. tell the employee that he should direct his criticism to the head of your agency if he wants quick action
   D. ask the employee if he has suggestions for revising the policy

KEY (CORRECT ANSWERS)

1.	C	11.	A	21.	C	31.	D
2.	B	12.	C	22.	C	32.	C
3.	B	13.	B	23.	C	33.	D
4.	D	14.	D	24.	B	34.	C
5.	A	15.	B	25.	A	35.	D
6.	C	16.	C	26.	A		
7.	D	17.	C	27.	B		
8.	A	18.	D	28.	D		
9.	A	19.	A	29.	D		
10.	B	20.	B	30.	C		

TEST 3

DIRECTIONS: Each question or incomplete statement is followed by several suggested answers or completions. Select the one that BEST answers the question or completes the statement. *PRINT THE LETTER OF THE CORRECT ANSWER IN THE SPACE AT THE RIGHT.*

1. At the request of your bureau head, you have designed a simple visitor's referral form. The form will be cut from 8½" x 11" stock. 1.____
Which of the following should be the dimensions of the form if you want to be sure that there is no waste of paper?
A. 2¾" x 4¼" B. 3¼" x 4¾" C. 3¾" x 4¾" D. 4½" x 5½"

2. An office contains six file cabinets, each containing three drawers. One of your responsibilities as a new Administrative Assistant is to see that there is sufficient filing space. At the present time, 1/4 of the file space contains forms, 2/9 contains personnel records, 1/3 contains reports, and 1/7 of the remaining space contains budget records. 2.____
If each drawer may contain more than one type of record, how much drawer space is now empty?
A. 0 drawers B. $^{13}/_{14}$ of a drawer
C. 3 drawers D. 3½ drawers

3. Assume that there were 21 working days in March. The five clerks in your unit had the following number of absences in March: 3.____
Clerk H: 2 absences
Clerk J: 1 absence
Clerk K: 6 absences
Clerk L: 0 absences
Clerk M: 10 absences
To the nearest day, what was the AVERAGE attendance in March for the five clerks in your unit?
A. 4 B. 17 C. 18 D. 21

Questions 4-12.

DIRECTIONS: Questions 4 through 12 each consist of a sentence which may or may not be an example of good English usage. Consider grammar, punctuation, spelling, capitalization, verbosity, awkwardness, etc. Examine each sentence, and then choose the CORRECT statement about it from the four choices below it. If the English usage in the sentence is better as given than with any of the changes suggested in options B, C, or D, choose option A.

4. The stenographers who are secretaries to commissioners have more varied duties than the stenographic pool. 4.____
   A. This is an example of effective writing.
   B. In this sentence there would be a comma after *commissioners* in order to break up the sentence into clauses.
   C. In this sentence, the words *stenographers in* should be inserted after the word "than".
   D. In this sentence, the word *commissioners* is misspelled.

5. A person who becomes an administrative assistant will be called upon to provide leadership, to insure proper quantity and quality of production, and many administrative chores must be performed. 5.____
   A. This sentence is an example of effective writing.
   B. The sentence should be divided into three separate sentences, each describing a duty.
   C. The words *many administrative chores must be performed* should be changed to *to perform many administrative chores.*
   D. The words *to provide leadership* should be changed to *to be a leader.*

6. A complete report has been submitted by our branch office, giving details about this transaction. 6.____
   A. This sentence is an example of effective writing.
   B. The phrase *giving details about this transaction* should be placed between the words *report* and *has.*
   C. A semi-colon should replace the comma after the word *office* to indicate independent clauses.
   D. A colon should replace the comma after the word *office* since the second clause provides further explanation.

7. The report was delayed because of the fact that the writer lost his rough draft two days before the deadline. 7.____
   A. This sentence is an example of effective writing.
   B. In this sentence the words *of the fact that* are unnecessary and should be deleted.
   C. In this sentence the words *because of the fact that* should be shortened to *due to.*
   D. In this sentence the word *before* should be replaced by *prior to.*

8. Included in this offer are a six months' guarantee, a complete set of instructions, and one free inspection of the equipment. 8.____
   A. This sentence is an example of effective writing.
   B. The word *is* should be substituted for the word *are.*
   C. The word *months* should have been spelled *month's.*
   D. The word *months* should be spelled *months.*

9. Certain employees come to the attention of their employers. Especially those with poor work records and excessive absences. 9.____
   A. This sentence is an example of effective writing.
   B. The period after the word *employers* should be changed to a comma, and the first letter of the word *Especially* should be changed to a small *e*.
   C. The period after the word *employers* should be changed to a semicolon, and the first letter of the word *Especially* should be changed to a small *e*.
   D. The period after the word *employers* should be changed to a colon.

10. The applicant had decided to decline the appointment by the time he was called for the interview. 10.____
   A. This sentence is an example of effective writing.
   B. In this sentence the word *had* should be deleted.
   C. In this sentence the phrase *was called* should be replaced by *had been called.*
   D. In this sentence the phrase *had decided to decline* should be replaced by *declined.*

11. There are two elevaters, each accommodating ten people 11.____
   A. This sentence is correct.
   B. In this sentence the word *elevaters* should be spelled *elevators.*
   C. In this sentence the word *each* should be replaced by the word *both.*
   D. In this sentence the word *accommodating* should be spelled *accomodating.*

12. With the aid of a special device, it was possible to alter the letterhead on the department's stationary. 12.____
   A. This sentence is correct.
   B. The word *aid* should be spelled *aide.*
   C. The word *device* should be spelled *devise.*
   D. The word *stationary* should be spelled *stationery.*

13. Examine the following sentence and then choose from the options below the correct word to be inserted in the blank space. 13.____
   Everybody in both offices _____ involved in the project.
   A. are B. feel C. is

Questions 14-18.

DIRECTIONS: Questions 14 through 18 are to be answered SOLELY on the basis of the information in the following passage.

A new way of looking at job performance promises to be a major advance in measuring and increasing a person's true effectiveness in business. The fact that individuals differ enormously in their judgment of when a piece of work is actually finished is significant. It is believed that more than half of all people in the business world are defective in the *sense of closure*, that is they do not know the proper time to throw the switch that turns off their effort in one direction and diverts it to a new job. Only a minority of workers at any level have the required judgment and the feeling of responsibility to work on a job to the point of maximum effectiveness. The vast majority let go of each task far short of the completion point.

Very often, a defective sense of closure exists in an entire staff. When that occurs, it usually stems from a long-standing laxness on the part of higher management. A low degree of responsibility has been accepted and ithas come to e standard. Combating this requires implementation of a few basic policies. Firstly, it is important to make each responsibility completely clear and to set certain guideposts as to what constitutes complete performance. Secondly, excuses for delays and failures should not be dealt with too sympathetically, but interest should be shown in the encountered obstacles. Lastly, a checklist should be used periodically to determine whether new levels of expectancy and new closure values have been set.

14. According to the above passage, a *majority of* people in the business world 14.____
    A. do not complete their work on time
    B. cannot properly determine when a particular job is completed
    C. make lame excuses for not completing a job on time
    D. can adequately judge their own effectiveness at work

15. It can be *inferred* from the above passage that when a poor sense of closure is observed among all the employees in a unit, the responsibility for raising the performance level belongs to 15.____
    A. non-supervisory employees
    B. the staff as a whole
    C. management
    D. first-line supervisors

16. It is *implied* by the above passage that, by the establishment of work guideposts, employees may develop a 16.____
    A. better understanding of expected performances
    B. greater interest in their work relationships
    C. defective sense of closure
    D. lower level of performance

17. It can be *inferred* from the above passage that an individual's idea of whether a job is finished is MOST closely associated with his 17.____
    A. loyalty to management
    B. desire to overcome obstacles
    C. ability to recognize his own defects
    D. sense of responsibility

18. Of the following, the BEST heading for the above passage is 18.____
    A. Management's Role in a Large Bureaucracy
    B. Knowing When a Job is Finished
    C. The Checklist, a Supervisor's Tool For Effectiveness
    D. Supervisory Techniques

Questions 19-25.

DIRECTIONS: Answer Questions 19 through 25 assuming that you are in charge of public information for an office which issues report and answers questions from other offices and from the public on changes in land use. The charts below represent comparative land use in four neighborhood. The area of each neighborhood is expressed in city blocks. Assume that all city blocks are the same size.

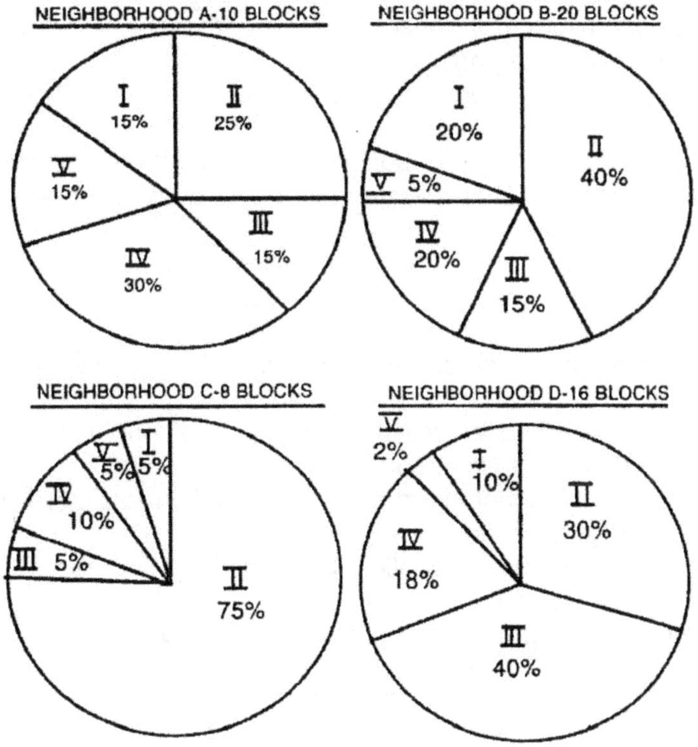

KEY: I – One- and two-family houses
II – Apartment buildings
III – Office buildings
IV – Retail stores
V - Factories and warehouses

19. In how many of these neighborhoods does residential use (categories I and II together) account for *more than 50%* of the land use? 19.____
A. 1 B. 2 C. 3 D. 4

20. How many of the neighborhoods have an area of land occupied by apartment buildings which is GREATER than the area of land occupied by apartment buildings in Neighborhood C? 20.____
A. None B. 1 C. 2 D. 3

21. Which neighborhood has the LARGEST land area occupied by factories and warehouses? 21.____
    A. A B. B C. C D. D

22. In which neighborhood is the LARGEST percentage of the land devoted to *both* office buildings and retail stores? 22.___
    A. A B. B C. C D. D

23. What is the difference, to the nearest city block, between the amount of land devoted to one- and two-family houses in Neighborhood A and the amount devoted to similar use in Neighborhood C? 23.____
    A. 1 block B. 2 blocks C. 5 blocks D. 10 blocks

24. Which one of the following types of buildings occupies the same amount of land area in Neighborhood B as the amount of land area occupied by retail stores in Neighborhood A? 24.____
    A. Apartment buildings B. Office buildings
    C. Retail stores D. Factories and warehouses

25. Based on the information in the charts, which one of the following statements must be TRUE? 25.____
    A. Factories and warehouses are gradually disappearing from all the neighborhoods except Neighborhood A.
    B. Neighborhood B has more land area occupied by retail stores than any of the other neighborhoods.
    C. There are more apartment dwellers living in Neighborhood C than in any of the other neighborhoods.
    D. All four of these neighborhoods are predominantly residential.

KEY (CORRECT ANSWERS)

1. A
2. C
3. B
4. C
5. C

6. B
7. B
8. A
9. B
10. A

11. B
12. D
13. C
14. B
15. C

16. A
17. D
18. B
19. B
20. B

21. A
22. D
23. A
24. B
25. B

SUPERVISION, ADMINISTRATION, MANAGEMENT, AND ORGANIZATION

EXAMINATION SECTION

TEST 1

DIRECTIONS: Each question or incomplete statement is followed by several suggested answers or completions. Select the one that BEST answers the question or completes the statement. *PRINT THE LETTER OF THE CORRECT ANSWER IN THE SPACE AT THE RIGHT.*

1. A supervisor scheduled and interview with a subordinate in order to discuss his unsatisfactory performance during the previous several weeks. The subordinate's work contained an excessive number of careless errors. After the interview, the supervisor, reviewing his own approach for self-examination, listed three techniques he had used in the interview, as follows: 1.____
   I. Specifically pointed out to the subordinate where he had failed to meet the standards expected.
   II. Shared the blame for certain management errors that had irritated the subordinate.
   III. Agreed with the subordinate on specific targets to be met during the period ahead.

   Of the following statements, the one that is MOST acceptable concerning the above three techniques is that
   A. all 3 techniques are correct
   B. techniques I and II are correct; III is not correct
   C. techniques II and III are correct; I is not correct
   D. techniques I and III are correct; II is not correct

2. Assume that the performance of an employee is not satisfactory. 2.____
   Of the following, the MOST effective way for a supervisor to attempt to improve the performance of the employee is to meet with him and to
   A. order him to change his behavior
   B. indicate the actions that are unsatisfactory and the penalties for them
   C. show him alternate ways of behaving and a method for him to evaluate his attempts at change
   D. suggest that he use the behavior of the supervisor as a model of acceptable conduct

3. Training employees to be productive workers is based on four fundamental principles: 3.____
   I. Demonstrate how the job should be done by telling and showing the correct operations step-by-step
   II. Allow the employee to get some of the feel of the job by allowing him to try it a bit
   III. Put him on the job while continuing to check his performance
   IV. Let him know why the job is important and why it must be done right

The MOST logical order for these training steps is:
A. I, III, II, IV B. I, IV, II, III C. II, I, III, IV D. IV, I, II, III

4. Sometimes a supervisor is faced with the need to train under-educated new employees. 4.____
The following five statements relate to training such employees.
I. Make the training general rather than specific
II. Rely upon demonstrations and illustrations whenever possible
III. Overtrain rather than undertrain by erring on the side of imparting a little more skill than is absolutely necessary
IV. Provide lots of follow-up on the job
V. Reassure and recognize frequently in order to increase self-confidence
Which of the following choices lists all the above statements that are generally CORRECT?
A. I, II, IV B. II, III, IV, V C. I, II, V D. I, II, IV, V

5. One of the ways in which some supervisors train subordinates is to discuss the subordinate's weaknesses with them. Experts who have explored the actual feelings and reactions of subordinates in such situations have come to the conclusion that such interviews USUALLY 5.____
A. are seen by subordinates as a threat to their self-esteem
B. give subordinates a feeling of importance which leads to better learning
C. convince subordinates to accept the opinion of the supervisor
D. result in the development of better supervision

6. The one of the following which BEST describes the rate at which a trainee learns departmental procedures is that he *probably* will learn 6.____
A. at the same rate throughout if the material to be learned is complex
B. slowly in the beginning and then learning will accelerate steadily
C. quickly for a while, than slow down temporarily
D. at the same rate if the material to be learned is lengthy

7. Which of the following statements concerning the delegation of work to subordinate employees is generally CORRECT? 7.____
A. A supervisor's personal attitude toward delegation has a minimal effect on his skill in delegating.
B. A willingness to let subordinates make mistakes has a place in work delegation.
C. The element of trust has little impact on the effectiveness of work delegation.
D. The establishment of controls does not enhance the process of delegation.

8. Assume that you are the chairman of a group that has been formed to discuss and solve a particular problem. After a half-hour of discussion, you feel that the group is wandering off the point and is no longer discussing the problem. 8.____
In this situation, it would be BEST for you to
A. wait to see whether the group will get back on the track by itself
B. ask the group to stop and to try a different approach

C. ask the group to stop, decide where they are going, and then to decide how to continue
D. ask the group to stop, decide where they are going, and then to continue in a different direction

9. One method of group decision-making is the use of committees. Following are four statements concerning committees. 9.____
I. Considering the value of each individual member's time, committees are costly.
II. One result of committee decisions is that no one may be held responsible for the decision.
III. Committees will make decisions more promptly than individuals.
IV. Committee decisions tend to be balanced and to take different viewpoints into account.
Which of the following choices lists all of the above statements that are generally CORRECT?
A. I and II B. II and III C. I, II, IV D. II, III, IV

10. Assume that an employee bypasses his supervisor and comes directly to you, the superior officer, to ask for a short leave of absence because of a pressing personal problem. The employee did not first consult with his immediate supervisor because he believes that his supervisor is unfavorably biased against him. 10.____
Of the following, the MOST desirable way for you to handle this situation is to
A. instruct the employee that is it not appropriate for him to go over the head of his supervisor regardless of their personal relationship
B. listen to a brief description of his problem and then tactfully suggest that he take the matter up with his supervisor before coming to you
C. request that both the employee and his supervisor meet jointly with you in order to discuss the employee's problem and to get at the reasons behind their apparent difficulty
D. listen carefully to the employee's problem and then, without committing yourself one way or the other, promise to discuss it with his supervisor

11. Which of the following statements concerning the motivation of subordinates is generally INCORRECT? The 11.____
A. authoritarian approach as the method of supervision is likely to result in the setting of minimal performance standards for themselves by subordinates
B. encouragement of competition among subordinates may lead to deterioration of teamwork
C. granting of benefits by a supervisor to subordinates in order to gain their gratitude will result in maximum output by the subordinates
D. opportunity to achieve job satisfaction has an important effect on motivating subordinates

12. Of the following, the MOST serious disadvantage of having a supervisor evaluate subordinates on the basis of measurable performance goals that are set jointly by the supervisor and the subordinates is that this results-oriented appraisal method 12.____
    A. focuses on past performance rather than plans for the future
    B. fails to provide sufficient feedback to help subordinates learn where they stand
    C. encourages the subordinates to conceal poor performance and set low goals
    D. changes the primary task of the supervisor from helping subordinates improve to criticizing their performance

13. A supervisor can BEST provide on-the-job satisfaction for his subordinates by 13.____
    A. providing rewards for good performance
    B. allowing them to decide when to do the assigned work
    C. motivating them to perform according to accepted procedures
    D. providing challenging work that achieves departmental objectives

14. Which of the following factors generally contributes MOST to job satisfaction among supervisory employees? 14.____
    A. Autonomy and independence on the job
    B. Job security
    C. Pleasant physical working conditions
    D. Adequate economic rewards

15. Large bureaucracies typically exhibit certain characteristics. 15.____
    Of the following, it would be CORRECT to state that such bureaucracies generally
    A. tend to oversimplify communications
    B. pay undue attention to informal organizations
    C. develop an attitude of "group-think" and conformity
    D. emphasize personal growth among employees

16. When positive methods fail to achieve conformity with accepted standards of conduct or performance, a negative type of action, punitive in nature, usually must follow. 16.____
    The one of the following that is usually considered LEAST important for the success of such punishment or negative discipline is that it be
    A. certain B. swift C. severe D. consistent

17. Assume that you are a supervisor. Philip Smith, who is under your supervision, informs you that James Jones, who is also your subordinate, has been creating antagonism and friction within the unit because of his unnecessarily gruff manner in dealing with his co-workers. Smith's remarks confirm your own observations of Jones' behavior and its effects. 17.____

In handling this situation, the one of the following procedures which will probably be MOST effective is to

A. ask Smith to act as an informal counselor to Jones and report the results to you
B. counsel the other employees in your unit on methods of changing attitudes of people
C. interview Jones and help him to understand this problem
D. order Jones to carry out his responsibilities with greater consideration for the feelings of his co-workers

18. The principle relating to the number of subordinates who can be supervised effectively by one supervisor is COMMONLY known as 18.____

A. span of control
B. delegation of authority
C. optimum personnel assignment
D. organizational factor

19. Ascertaining and improving the level of morale in a public agency is one of the responsibilities of a conscientious supervisor. 19.____
The one of the following aspects of subordinates' behavior which is NOT an indication of low morale is

A. lower-level employees participating in organizational decision-making
B. careless treatment of equipment
C. general deterioration of personal appearance
D. formation of cliques

20. Employees may resist changes in agency operations even though such changes are often necessary. If you, as a supervisor, are attempting to introduce a necessary change, you should first fully explain the reasons for it to your staff. 20.____
Your NEXT step should be to

A. set specific goals and outline programs for all employees
B. invite employee participation in effectuating the change by asking for suggestions to accomplish it
C. discuss the need for improved work performance by city employees
D. point out the penalties for non-cooperation without singling out any employee by name

21. A supervisor should normally void giving orders in an offhand or casual manner MAINLY because his subordinates 21.____

A. are like most people and may resent being treated lightly
B. may attach little importance to these orders
C. may work best if given the choice of work methods
D. are unlikely to need instructions in most matters

22. Assume that, as a supervisor, you have just praised a subordinate. While he expresses satisfaction at your praise, he complains that it does not help him get promoted even though he is on a promotion eligible list, since there is no current vacancy. 22.____

In these circumstances, it would be BEST for you to

A. minimize the importance of advancement and emphasize the satisfaction in the work itself
B. follow up by pointing out some errors he has committed in the past
C. admit that the situation exists, and express the hope that it will improve
D. tell him that, until quite recently, advancement was even slower

23. Departmental policies are usually broad rules or guides for action. It is important for a supervisor to understand his role with respect to policy implementation. 23.____
Of the following, the MOST accurate description of this role is that a supervisor should

A. be apologetic toward his subordinates when applying unpopular policies to them
B. act within policy limits, although he can attempt to influence policy change by making his thoughts and observations known to his superior
C. arrange his activities so that he is able to deal simultaneously with situations that involve several policy matters
D. refrain as much as possible from exercising permissible discretion in applying policy to matters under his control

24. A supervisor should be aware that most subordinates will ask questions at meetings or group discussions in order to 24.____

A. stimulate other employees to express their opinions
B discover how they may be affected by the subjects under discussion
C. display their knowledge of the topics under discussion
D. consume time in order to avoid returning to their normal tasks

25. Don't assign responsibilities with conflicting objectives to the same work group. For example, to require a unit to monitor the quality of its own work is a bad practice. 25.____
This practice is MOST likely to be bad because

A. the chain of command will be unnecessarily lengthened
B. it is difficult to portray mixed duties accurately on an organization chart
C. employees may act in collusion to cover up poor work
D. the supervisor may delegate responsibilities which he should retain

KEY (CORRECT ANSWERS)

1.	A	11.	C
2.	C	12.	C
3.	D	13.	D
4.	B	14.	A
5.	A	15.	C
6.	C	16.	C
7.	B	17.	C
8.	C	18.	A
9.	C	19.	A
10.	D	20.	B

21.	B
22.	C
23.	B
24.	B
25.	C

TEST 2

DIRECTIONS: Each question or incomplete statement is followed by several suggested answers or completions. Select the one that BEST answers the question or completes the statement. *PRINT THE LETTER OF THE CORRECT ANSWER IN THE SPACE AT THE RIGHT.*

1. Some supervisors use an approach in which each phase of the job is explained in broad terms supervision is general, and employees are allowed broad discretion in performing their job duties. 1.____
   Such a supervisory approach USUALLY affects employee motivation by
   A. improving morale and providing an incentive to work harder
   B. providing little or no incentive to work harder than the minimum required
   C. creating extra pressure, usually resulting in decreased performance
   D. reducing incentive to work and causing employees to feel neglected, particularly in performing complex tasks

2. An employee complains to a superior officer that he has been treated unfairly by his supervisor, stating that other employees have been given less work to do and shown other forms of favoritism. 2.____
   Of the following, the BEST thing for the superior officer to do FIRST in order to handle this problem is to
   A. try to discover whether the subordinate has a valid complaint or if something else is the real problem
   B. ask other employees whether they feel their treatment is consistent and fair
   C. ask his supervisor to explain the charges
   D. see that the number of cases assigned to this employee is reduced

3. Of the following, the MOST important condition needed to help a group of people to work well together and get the job done is 3.____
   A. higher salaries and a better working environment
   B. enough free time to relieve the tension
   C. good communication among everyone involved in the job
   D. assurance that everyone likes the work

4. A supervisor realizes that a subordinate has called in sick for three Mondays out of the past four. These absences have interfered with staff performance and have been part of the cause of the unit's "behind schedule" condition. 4.____
   In order to correct this situation, it would be BEST for the supervisor to
   A. order the subordinate to explain his abuse of sick leave
   B. discuss with the subordinate the penalties for abusing sick leave
   C. discuss the matter with his own supervisor
   D. ask the subordinate in private whether he has a problem about coming to work

5. Of the following, the MOST effective way for a supervisor to minimize undesirable rumors about new policies in the units under his supervision is to 5.____
   A. bypass the supervisor and communicate directly with the individual members of the units
   B. supply immediate and accurate information to everyone who is supposed to be informed
   C. play down the importance of the rumors
   D. issue all communications in written form

6. Which of the following is an indication that a superior officer is delegating authority PROPERLY? 6.____
   A. The superior officer closely checks the work of experienced subordinates at all stages in order to maintain standards.
   B. The superior officer gives overlapping assignments to insure that work is completed on time.
   C. The work of his subordinates can proceed and be completed during the superior officer's absence.
   D. The work of each supervisor is reviewed by him more than once in order to insure quality.

7. Of the following supervisory practices, the one which is MOST likely to foster employee morale is for the supervisor to 7.____
   A. take an active interest in subordinates' personal lives
   B. ignore mistakes
   C. give praise when justified
   D. permit rules to go unenforced occasionally

8. As the supervisor who is responsible for the implementation of new paperwork procedure, you note that the workers often do not follow the stipulated procedure. 8.____
   Before taking action, it would be ADVISABLE to realize that
   A. unconscious behavior, such as failure to adapt to change, is largely uncontrollable
   B. new procedures sometimes have to be modified and adapted after being tried out
   C. threats of disciplinary action will encourage approval of change
   D. procedures that fail should be abandoned and replaced

9. The one of the following which is generally considered to be the MOST significant criticism of the modern practice of effective human relations in management of large organizations is that human relations 9.____
   A. weakens management authority over employees
   B. gives employees control of operations
   C. can be used to manipulate and control employees
   D. weakens unions

10. Of the following, the MOST important reason why the supervisor should promote good supervisor-subordinate relations is to encourage his staff to 10.____
    A. feel important
    B. be more receptive to control
    C. be happy in their work
    D. meet production performance levels

11. A superior officer decides to assign a special report directly to an employee, bypassing his supervisor. 11.____
    In general, this practice is
    A. *advisable*, chiefly because it broadens the superior officer's span of authority
    B. *inadvisable*, chiefly because it undermines the authority of the supervisor in the eyes of his subordinates
    C. *advisable*, chiefly because it reduces the number of details the supervisor must know
    D. *inadvisable*, chiefly because it gives too much work to the employee

12. Many supervisors make it a practice to solicit suggestions from their subordinates and to encourage their participation in decision-making. 12.____
    The success of this type of supervision usually depends MOST directly upon the
    A. quality of leadership provided by the supervisor
    B. number of the supervisor's immediate subordinates
    C. availability of opportunities for employee advancement
    D. degree to which work assignments cause problems

13. Small informal groups or "cliques" often appear in a work setting. 13.____
    The one of the following which is generally an advantage of such groups, from an administrative point of view, is that they
    A. are not influenced by the administrative set-up of the office
    B. encourage socializing after working hours
    C. develop leadership roles among the office staff
    D. provide a "steam valve" for release of tension and fatigue

14. Assume that you are a superior officer in charge of several supervisors who, in turn, are in charge of a number of employees. The employees who are supervised by Jones (a supervisor) come as a group to you and indicate several reasons why Jones is incompetent and "has to go." 14.____
    Of the following, your BEST course of action to take FIRST is to
    A. direct the employees to see Jones about the matter
    B. suggest to the employees that they should attempt to work with Jones until he can be transferred
    C. discuss the possibility of terminating Jones with your superior
    D. ask Jones about the comments of the employees after they depart

15. Of the following, the MAIN effect which the delegation of authority can have on the efficiency of an organization is to 15.____
   A. reduce the risk of decision-making errors
   B. produce uniformity of policy and action
   C. facilitate speedier decisions and actions
   D. enable closer control of operations

16. Of the following, the main DISADVANTAGE of temporarily transferring a newly appointed worker to another unit because of an unexpected vacancy is that the temporary nature of his assignment will, MOST likely, 16.____
   A. undermine his incentive to orient himself to his new job
   B. interfere with his opportunities for future advancement
   C. result in friction between himself and his new co-workers
   D. place his new supervisor in a difficult and awkward position

17. Assume that you, as a supervisor, have decided to raise the quality of work produced by your subordinates. 17.____
   The BEST of the following procedures for you to follow is to
   A. develop mathematically precise standards
   B. appoint a committee of subordinates to set firm and exacting guidelines, including penalties for deviations
   C. modify standards developed by supervisors in other organizations
   D. provide consistent evaluation of subordinates' work, furnishing training whenever advisable

18. Assume that a supervisor under your supervision strongly objects whenever changes are proposed which would improve the efficiency of his unit. 18.____
   Of the following, the MOST desirable way for you to change his attitude is to
   A. involve him in the planning and formulation of changes
   B. promise to recommend him for a more challenging assignment if he accepts changes
   C. threaten to have him transferred to another unit if he does not accept changes
   D. ask him to go along with the changes on a tentative, trial basis

19. Work goals may be defined in terms of units produced or in terms of standards of performance. 19.____
   Which of the following statements concerning work goals is CORRECT?
   A. Workers who have a share in establishing goals tend to set a fairly high standard for themselves, but fail to work toward it.
   B. Workers tend to produce according to what they believe are the goals actually expected of them.
   C. Since workers usually produce less than the established goals, management should set goals higher than necessary.
   D. The individual differences of workers can be minimized by using strict goals and invariable procedures.

20. Of the following, the type of employee who would respond BEST to verbal instructions given in the form of a suggestion or wish is the 20.____
    A. experienced worker who is eager to please
    B. sensitive and emotional worker
    C. hostile worker who is somewhat lazy
    D. slow and methodical worker

21. As a supervisor, you note that the output of an experienced staff member has dropped dramatically during the last two months. In addition, his error rate is significantly above that of other staff members. When you ask the employee the reason for his poor performance, he says, "Well, it's rather personal and I would rather not talk about it if you don't mind." 21.____
    At this point, which of the following would be the BEST reply?
    A. Tell him that you will give him two weeks to improve or you will discuss the matter with your own supervisor
    B. Insist that he tell you the reason for his poor work and assure him that anything personal will be kept confidential
    C. Say that you don't want to interfere, but, at the same time, his work has deteriorated, and that you're concerned about it
    D. Explain in a friendly manner that you are going to place a warning letter in his personnel folder that states he has one month in which to improve

22. Research studies have shown that employees who are strongly interested in achievement and advancement on the job usually want assignments where the chance of success is _____, and desire _____ supervisory evaluation of their performance. 22.____
    A. low; frequent
    B. high; general
    C. high; infrequent
    D. moderate; specific

23. Of the following, a function of the supervisor that concerns itself with the process of determining a course of action from alternatives is USUALLY referred to as 23.____
    A. decentralization
    B. planning
    C. controlling
    D. input

24. Favorable working conditions are an important variable in producing an effective work unit. 24.____
    Which of the following would be LEAST conducive in providing a favorable work situation?
    A. Applying a job enrichment program to a routine clerical position
    B. Setting practical goals for the work unit which are consistent with the overall objective of the agency
    C. Assigning individuals to positions which require a higher level of educational achievement than that which they possess
    D. Establishing a communications system which distributes information and provides feedback to all organizational levels

25. Ever supervisor within an organization should know to whom he reports and who reports to him. 25.____
Within the organization, this will MOST likely insure
   A. unity of command
   B. confidentiality of sensitive issues
   C. excellent morale
   D. the elimination of the grapevine

KEY (CORRECT ANSWERS)

1.	A	11.	B
2.	A	12.	A
3.	C	13.	D
4.	D	14.	D
5.	B	15.	C
6.	C	16.	A
7.	C	17.	D
8.	B	18.	A
9.	C	19.	B
10.	D	20.	A

21. C
22. D
23. B
24. C
25. A

TEST 3

DIRECTIONS: Each question or incomplete statement is followed by several suggested answers or completions. Select the one that BEST answers the question or completes the statement. *PRINT THE LETTER OF THE CORRECT ANSWER IN THE SPACE AT THE RIGHT.*

1. In trying to improve the motivation of his subordinates, a supervisor can achieve the BEST results by taking action based upon the assumption that *most* employees 1.____
   A. have an inherent dislike of work
   B. wish to be closely directed
   C. are more interested in security than in assuming responsibility
   D. will exercise self-direction without coercion

2. Supervisors in public departments have many functions. 2.____
   Of the following, the function which is LEAST appropriate for a supervisor is to
   A. serve as a deputy for the administrator within his own unit
   B. determine needs within his unit and plan programs to meet these needs
   C. supervise, train, and evaluate all personnel assigned to his unit
   D. initiate and carry out fundraising projects, such as bazaars and carnivals, to buy needed equipment

3. When there are conflicts or tensions between top management and lower-level employees in any public department, the supervisor should FIRSTS attempt to 3.____
   A. represent and enforce the management point of view
   B. act as the representative of the workers to get their ideas across to management
   C. serve as a two-way spokesman, trying to interpret each side to the other
   D. remain neutral, but keep informed of changes in the situation

4. A probationary period for new employees is usually provided in public agencies. 4.____
   The MAJOR purpose of such a period is usually to
   A. allow a determination of employee's suitability for the position
   B. obtain evidence as to employee's ability to perform in a higher position
   C. conform to requirement that ethnic hiring goals be met for all positions
   D. train the new employee in the duties of the position

5. An effective program of orientation for new employees usually includes all of the following EXCEPT 5.____
   A. having the supervisor introduce the new employee to his job, outlining his responsibilities and how to carry them out
   B. permitting the new worker to tour the facility or department, so he can observe all parts of it in action
   C. scheduling meetings for new employees, at which the job requirements are explained to them and they are given personnel manuals
   D. testing the new worker on his skills, and sending him to a centralized in-service workshop

6. In-service training is an important responsibility of supervisors. 6.____
The MAJOR reason for such training is to
   A. avoid future grievance procedures, because employees might say they were not prepared to carry out their jobs
   B. maximize the effectiveness of the department by helping each employee perform at his full potential
   C. satisfy inspection teams from central headquarters of the department
   D. help prevent disagreements with members of the community

7. There are many forms of useful in-service training. 7.____
Of the following, the training method which is NOT an appropriate technique for leadership development is to
   A. provide special workshops or clinics in activity skills
   B. conduct pre-season institutes to familiarize new workers with the program of the department and with their roles
   C. schedule team meetings for problem-solving, including both supervisors and leaders
   D. have the leader rate himself on an evaluation form periodically

8. Of the following techniques of evaluating work training programs, the one that is BEST is to 8.____
   A pass out a carefully designed questionnaire to the trainees at the completion of the program
   B. test the knowledge that trainees have both at the beginning of training and at its completion
   C. interview the trainees at the completion of the program
   D. evaluate performance before and after training for both a control group and an experimental group

9. Assume that a new supervisor is having difficulty making his instructions to subordinates clearly understood. 9.____
The one of the following which is the FIRST step he should take in dealing with this problem is to
   A. set up a training workshop in communication skills
   B. determine the extent and nature of the communication gap
   C. repeat both verbal and written instructions several times
   D. simplify his written and spoken vocabulary

10. Discipline of employees is usually a supervisor's responsibility. There may be several useful forms of disciplinary action in public employment. 10.____
Of the following, the form that is LEAST appropriate is the
   A. written reprimand or warning
   B. involuntary transfer to another work setting
   C. demotion or suspension
   D. assignment of added hours of work each week

11. Of the following, the MOST effective means of dealing with employee disciplinary problems is to 11.____
    A. give personality tests to individuals to identify their psychological problems
    B. distribute and discuss a policy manual containing exact rules governing employee behavior
    C. establish a single, clear penalty to be imposed for all wrongdoing irrespective of degree
    D. have supervisors get to know employees well through social mingling

12. A recently developed technique for appraising work performance is to have the supervisor record on a continual basis all significant incidents in each subordinate's behavior that indicate unsuccessful action and those that indicate poor behavior. 12.____
    Of the following, a major DISADVANTAGE of this method of performance appraisal is that it
    A. often leads to overly close supervision
    B. results in competition among those subordinates being evaluated
    C. tends to result in superficial judgments
    D. lacks objectivity for evaluating performance

13. Assume that you are a supervisor and have observed the performance of an employee during a period of time. You have concluded that his performance needs improvement. 13.____
    In order to approve his performance, it would, therefore, be BEST for you to
    A. note your findings in the employee's personnel folder so that his behavior is a matter of record
    B. report the findings to the personnel officer so he can take prompt action
    C. schedule a problem-solving conference with the employee
    D. recommend his transfer to simpler duties

14. When an employee's absences or latenesses seem to be nearing excessiveness, the supervisor should speak with him to find out what the problem is. 14.____
    Of the following, if such a discussion produces no reasonable explanation, the discussion usually BEST serves to
    A. affirm clearly the supervisor's adherence to proper policy
    B. alert other employees that such behavior is unacceptable
    C. demonstrate that the supervisor truly represents higher management
    D. notify the employee that his behavior is being observed and evaluated

15. Assume that an employee willfully and recklessly violates an important agency regulation. The nature of the violation is of such magnitude that it demands immediate action, but the facts of the case are not entirely clear. Further assume that the supervisor is free to make any of the following recommendations. 15.____

The MOST appropriate action for the supervisor to take is to recommend that the employee be
A. discharged B. suspended C. forced to resign D. transferred

16. Although employees' titles may be identical, each position in that title may be considerably different.
Of the following, a supervisor should carefully assign each employee to a specific position based PRIMARILY on the employee's 16.____
A. capability B. experience C. education D. seniority

17. The one of the following situations where it is MOST appropriate to transfer an employee to a *similar* assignment is one in which the employee 17.____
A. lacks motivation and interest
B. experiences a personality conflict with his supervisor
C. is negligent in the performance of his duties
D. lacks capacity or ability to perform assigned tasks

18. The one of the following which is LEAST likely to be affected by improvement in the morale of personnel is employee 18.____
A. skill B. absenteeism C. turnover D. job satisfaction

19. The one of the following situations in which it is LEAST appropriate for a supervisor to delegate authority to subordinates is where the supervisor 19.____
A. lacks confidence in his own abilities to perform certain work
B. is overburdened and cannot handle all his responsibilities
C. refers all disciplinary problems to his subordinate
D. has to deal with an emergency or crisis

20. Of the following, the BEST attitude toward the use of volunteers in programs is that volunteers should be 20.____
A. discouraged, since they cannot be depended upon to show up regularly
B. employed as a last resort when paid personnel are unavailable
C. seen as an appropriate means of providing leadership, when effectively recruited and supervised
D. eliminated to raise the professionalism of personnel

21. A supervisor finds that he is spending too much time on routine tasks, and not enough time on coordinating the work of his employees.
It would be MOST advisable for this supervisor to 21.____
A. delegate the task of work coordination to a capable subordinate
B. eliminate some of the routine tasks that the unit is required to perform
C. assign some of the routine tasks to his subordinates
D. postpone the performance of routine tasks until he has achieved proper coordination of his employees' work

22. Of the following, the MOST important reason for having an office manual in looseleaf form rather than in permanent binding is that the looseleaf form 22.____
    A. facilitates the addition of new material and the removal of obsolete material
    B. permits several people to use different sections of the manual at the same time
    C. is less expensive to prepare than permanent binding
    D. is more durable than permanent binding

23. In his first discussion with a newly appointed employee, the LEAST important of the following topics for a supervisor of a unit to include is the 23.____
    A. duties the subordinate is expected to perform on the job
    B. functions of the unit
    C. methods of determining standards of performance
    D. nature and duration of the training the subordinate will receive on the job

24. A supervisor has just been told by a subordinate, Mr. Jones, that another employee, Mr. Smith, deliberately disobeyed an important rule of the department by taking home some confidential departmental material. 24.____
    Of the following courses of action, it would be MOST advisable for the supervisor FIRST to
    A. discuss the matter privately, with both Mr. Jones and Mr. Smith at the same time
    B. call a meeting of the entire staff and discuss the matter generally without mentioning any employee by name
    C. arrange to supervise Mr. Smith's activities more closely
    D. discuss the matter privately with Mr. Smith

25. The one of the following actions which would be MOST efficient and economical for a supervisor to take to minimize the effect of seasonal fluctuations in the workload of his unit is to 25.____
    A. increase his permanent staff until it is large enough to handle the work of the busy season
    B. request the purchase of time and labor-saving equipment to be used primarily during the busy season
    C. lower, temporarily, the standards for quality of work performance during peak loads
    D. schedule for the slow season work that it is not essential to perform during the busy season

KEY (CORRECT ANSWERS)

1. D
2. D
3. C
4. A
5. D

6. B
7. D
8. D
9. B
10. D

11. B
12. A
13. C
14. D
15. B

16. A
17. B
18. A
19. C
20. C

21. C
22. A
23. C
24. D
25. D

TEST 4

DIRECTIONS: Each question or incomplete statement is followed by several suggested answers or completions. Select the one that BEST answers the question or completes the statement. *PRINT THE LETTER OF THE CORRECT ANSWER IN THE SPACE AT THE RIGHT.*

1. Assume that, while instructing a worker on a new procedure, the instructor asks, at frequent intervals, whether there are any questions. 1.____
His asking for questions is a
   A. *good practice*, because it affords the worker an opportunity to participate actively in the lesson
   B. *good practice*, because it may reveal points that are not understood by the worker
   C. *poor practice*, because workers generally find it embarrassing to ask questions
   D. *poor practice*, because it may result in wasting time on irrelevant matters

2. Any person thoroughly familiar with the specific steps in a particular type of work is well-qualified to serve as a training course instructor in the work. 2.____
This statement is *erroneous* CHIEFLY because
   A. a qualified instructor cannot be expected to have detailed information about many specific fields
   B. a person who knows a field thoroughly may not be good at passing his knowledge along to others
   C. it is practically impossible for any instructor to be acquainted with all the specific steps in a particular type of work
   D. what is true of one type of work is not necessarily true of other types of work

3. Of the following traits, the one that is LEAST essential for the "ideal" supervisor is that she 3.____
   A. be consistent in her interpretation of the rules and policies of the agency for which she works
   B. is able to judge a person's ability at her first meeting with that person
   C. know her own job thoroughly
   D. appreciate and acknowledge honest effort and above-average work

4. The one of the following which is generally the basic reason for using standard procedure is to 4.____
   A. serve as a basis for formulating policies
   B. provide the sequence of steps for handling recurring activities
   C. train new employees in the policies and objectives
   D. facilitate periodic review of standard practices

5. An employee, while working at the bookkeeping machine, accidentally kicks off the holdup alarm system. She notifies the supervisor that she can hear the holdup alarm bell ringing, and requests that the holdup alarm system be reset. After the holdup alarm system has been reset, the supervisor should notify the manager that the alarm 5.____
   A. is in proper working order
   B. should be shut off while the employee is working the bookkeeping machine to avoid another such accident
   C. kick-plate should be moved away from the worker's reception window so that it cannot be set off accidentally
   D. should be relocated so that it cannot be heard in the bookkeeping office

6. A supervisor who spends a considerate amount of time correcting subordinates' procedural errors should consider FIRST the possibility of 6.____
   A. disciplining those who make errors consistently
   B. instituting refresher training sessions
   C. redesigning work forms
   D. requesting that the requirements for entry-level jobs be changed

7. A supervisor has a subordinate who has been late the past four mornings. Of the following, the MOST important action for the supervisor to take FIRST is to 7.____
   A. read the rules concerning lateness to the employee in an authoritative manner
   B. give the subordinate a chance to explain the reason for his lateness
   C. tell the employee he must come in on time the next day
   D. ask the friends of the employee whether they can tell him the reason for the employee's lateness

8. During a conversation, a subordinate tells his supervisor about a family problem For the supervisor to give EXPLICIT advice to the subordinate would be 8.____
   A. *desirable*, primarily because a happy employee is more likely to be productive
   B. *undesirable*, primarily because the supervisor should not allow a subordinate to discuss personal problems
   C. *desirable*, primarily because their personal relations will show a marked improvement
   D. *undesirable*, primarily because a supervisor should not take responsibility for handling a subordinate's personal problem

9. As a supervisor, you have received instructions for a drastic change in the procedure for processing cases. Of the following, the approach which is MOST likely to result in acceptance of the change by your subordinates is for you to 9.____
   A. inform all subordinates of the change by written memo so that they will have guidelines to follow
   B. ask your superior to inform the unit members about the change at a staff meeting

C. recruit the most experienced employee in the unit to give individual instruction to the other unit members
D. discuss the change and the reasons for it with the staff so that they understand their role in its implementation

10. Of the following, the principle which should GENERALLY guide a supervisor in the training of employees under his supervision is that 10.____
A. training of employees should be delegated to more experienced employees in the same title
B. primary emphasis should be placed on training for future assignments
C. the training process should be a highly individual matter
D. training efforts should concentrate on employees who have the greatest potential

KEY (CORRECT ANSWERS)

1.	B	6.	B
2.	B	7.	B
3.	B	8.	D
4.	B	9.	D
5.	D	10.	C

SUPERVISION, ADMINISTRATION, MANAGEMENT AND ORGANIZATION

EXAMINATION SECTION

TEST 1

DIRECTIONS: Each question or incomplete statement is followed by several suggested answers or completions. Select the one that BEST answers the question or completes the statement. *PRINT THE LETTER OF THE CORRECT ANSWER IN THE SPACE AT THE RIGHT.*

1. The one of the following practices by a supervisor which is MOST likely to lead to confusion and inefficiency is for him to 1.____
   A. give orders verbally directly to the man assigned to the job
   B. issue orders only in writing
   C. follow up his orders after issuing them
   D. relay his orders to the men through co-workers

2. If you are given an oral order by a supervisor which you do not understand completely, you should 2.____
   A. use your own judgment
   B. discuss the order with your men
   C. ask your supervisor for a further explanation
   D. carry out that part of the order which you do understand and then ask for more information

3. An orientation program for a group of new employees should NOT ordinarily include a 3.____
   A. review of the organizational structure of the agency
   B. detailed description of the duties of each new employee
   C. description of the physical layout of the repair shop
   D. statement of the rules pertaining to sick leave, vacation, and holidays

4. The MOST important rule to follow with regard to discipline is that a man should be disciplined 4.____
   A. after everyone has had time to "cool off"
   B. as soon as possible after the infraction of rules
   C. only for serious rule violations
   D. before he makes a mistake

5. If the men under your supervision continue to work effectively even when you are out sick for several days, it would MOST probably indicate that 5.____
   A. the men are merely trying to show you up
   B. the men are in constant fear of you and are glad you are away
   C. you have trained your men properly and have their full cooperation
   D. you are serving no useful purpose since the men can get along without you

6. When evaluating subordinates, the employee who should be rated HIGHEST by his supervisor is the one who 6.____
   A. never lets the supervisor do heavy lifting
   B. asks many questions about the work
   C. makes many suggestions on work procedures
   D. listens to instructions and carries them out

7. Of the following, the factor which is generally MOST important to the conduct of successful training is 7.____
   A. time B. preparation C. equipment D. space

8. One of the MAJOR disadvantages of "on-the-job" training is that it 8.____
   A. requires a long training period for instructors
   B. may not be progressive
   C. requires additional equipment
   D. may result in the waste of supplies

9. For a supervisor to train workers in several trades which involve various skills, presents many training problems. 9.____
   The one of the following which is NOT true in such a training situation is that
   A. less supervision is required
   B. greater planning for training is required
   C. rotation of assignments is necessary
   D. less productivity can be expected

10. For a supervisor of repair workers to have each worker specialize in learning a single trade is GENERALLY 10.____
    A. *desirable*; each worker will become expert in his assigned trade
    B. *undesirable*; there is less flexibility of assignments possible when each worker has learned only a single trade
    C. *desirable*; the training responsibility of the supervisor is simplified when each worker is required to learn a single trade
    D. *undesirable*; workers lose interest quickly when they know they are expected to learn a single trade

11. An IMPORTANT advantage of standardizing work procedures is that it 11.____
    A. develops all-around skills
    B. makes the work less monotonous
    C. provides an incentive for good work
    D. enable the work to be done with less supervision

12. Generally, the GREATEST difficulty in introducing new work methods is due to the fact that 12.____
    A. men become set in their ways
    B. the old way is generally better
    C. only the department will benefit from changes
    D. explaining new methods is time consuming

13. Assume that you are required to transmit an order with, which you do not agree, to your subordinates. 13.____
In this case, it would be BEST for you to
A. ask one of your superiors to transmit the order
B. refuse to transmit an order with which you do not agree
C. transmit the order but be sure to explain that you do not agree with it
D. transmit the order and enforce it to the best of your ability

14. The MAIN reason for written orders is that 14.____
A. proper blame can be placed if the order is not carried out
B. the order will be carried out faster
C. the order can be properly analyzed as to its meaning
D. there will be no doubt as to what the order says

15. You have been informed unofficially by another shop manager that some of the men under your supervision are loafing on the job. 15.____
This situation can be BEST handled by
A. telling the man to mind his own business
B. calling the men together and reprimanding them
C. having the men work under your direct supervision
D. arranging to make spot checks at more frequent intervals

16. Suggestions on improving methods of doing work, when submitted by a new employee, should be 16.____
A. examined for possible merit because the new man may have a fresh viewpoint
B. ignored because it would make the old employees resentful
C. disregarded because he is too unfamiliar with the work
D. examined only for the purpose of judging the new man

17. One of your employees often slows down the work of his crew by playing practical jokes. 17.____
The BEST way to handle this situation is to
A. arrange for his assignment to more than his share of unpleasant jobs
B. warn him that he must stop this practice at once
C. ignore this situation for he will soon tire of it
D. ask your supervisor to transfer him

18. One of your men is always complaining about working conditions, equipment, and his fellow workers. 18.____
The BEST action for you to take in this situation is to
A. have this man work alone if possible
B. consider each complaint on is merits
C. tell him bluntly that you will not listen to any of his complaints
D. give this man the worst jobs until he quits complaining

19. It is generally agreed that men who are interested in their work will do the best work. 19.____
A supervisor can LEAST stimulate this interest by
   A. complimenting men on good work
   B. correcting men on their working procedures
   C. striving to create overtime for his men
   D. recommending merit raises for excellent work

20. If you, as a supervisor, have criticized one of your men for making a mistake, you should 20.____
   A. remind the man of his error from time to time to keep him on his toes
   B. overlook any further errors which this man may make, otherwise he may feel he is a victim of discrimination
   C. give the man the opportunity to redeem himself
   D. impress the man with the fact that all his work will be closely checked from then on

21. In his efforts to maintain standards of performance, a shop manager uses a system of close supervision to detect or catch errors. 21.____
An *opposite* method of accomplishing the *same* objective is to employ a program which
   A. instills in each employee a pride of workmanship to do the job correctly the first time
   B. groups each job accordingly to the importance to the overall objectives of the program
   C. makes the control of quality the responsibility of an inspector
   D. emphasizes that there is a "one" best way for an employee to do s specific job

22. Assume that after taking over a repair shop, a shop manager feels that he is taking too much time maintaining records. 22.____
He should
   A. temporarily assign this job to one of his senior repair crew chiefs
   B. get together with his supervisor to determine if all these records are needed
   C. stop keeping those records which he believes are unnecessary
   D. spend a few additional hours each day until his records are current

23. In order to apply performance standards to employees engaged in repair shop activities, a shop manager must FIRST 23.____
   A. allow workers to decide for themselves the way to do the job
   B. determine what is acceptable as satisfactory work
   C. separate the more difficult tasks from the simpler tasks
   D. stick to an established work schedule

24. Of the following actions a shop manager can take to determine whether the vehicles used in his shop are being utilized properly, the one which will give him the LEAST meaningful information is 24.____
   A. conducting an analysis of vehicle assignments
   B. reviewing the number of miles traveled by each vehicle with and without loads
   C. recording the unloaded weights of each vehicle
   D. comparing the amount of time vehicles are parked at job sites with the time required to travel to and from job sites

25. For a shop manager, the MOST important reason that equipment which is used infrequently should be considered for disposal is that 25.____
   A. the time required for its maintenance could be better used elsewhere
   B. such equipment may cause higher management to think that your shop is not busy
   C. the men may resent having to work on such equipment
   D. such equipment usually has a higher breakdown rate in operation

KEY (CORRECT ANSWERS)

1.	D	11.	D
2.	C	12.	A
3.	B	13.	D
4.	B	14.	D
5.	C	15.	D
6.	D	16.	A
7.	B	17.	B
8.	B	18.	B
9.	A	19.	C
10.	B	20.	C

21.	A
22.	B
23.	B
24.	C
25.	A

TEST 2

DIRECTIONS: Each question or incomplete statement is followed by several suggested answers or completions. Select the one that BEST answers the question or completes the statement. *PRINT THE LETTER OF THE CORRECT ANSWER IN THE SPACE AT THE RIGHT.*

1. Assume that one of your subordinates approaches you with a grievance concerning working conditions. 1.____
Of the following, the BEST action for you to take first is to
   A. "soft-soap" him, since most grievances are imaginary
   B. settle the grievance to his satisfaction
   C. try to talk him out of his complaint
   D. listen patiently and sincerely to the complaint

2. Of the following, the BEST way for a supervisor to help a subordinate learn a new skill which requires the use of tools is for him to give this subordinate 2.____
   A. a list of good books on the subject
   B. lectures on the theoretical aspects of the task
   C. opportunities to watch someone using the tools
   D. opportunities to practice the skill, under close supervision

3. A supervisor finds that his own work load is excessive because several of his subordinates are unable to complete their assignments. 3.____
Of the following, the BEST action for him to take to improve this situation is to
   A. discipline these subordinates
   B. work overtime
   C. request additional staff
   D. train these subordinates in more efficient work methods

4. The one of the following situations which is MOST likely to be the result of *poor* morale is a(n) 4.____
   A. high rate of turnover
   B. decrease in number of requests by subordinates for transfers
   C. increase in the backlog of work
   D. decrease in the rate of absenteeism

5. As a supervisor, you find that several of your subordinates are not meeting their deadlines because they are doing work assigned to them by one of your fellow supervisors without your knowledge. 5.____
Of the following, the BEST course of action for you to take in this situation is to
   A. tell the other supervisors to make future assignments through you
   B. assert your authority by publicly telling the other supervisors to stop issuing orders to your workers
   C. go along with this practice; it is an effective way to fully utilize the available manpower
   D. take the matter directly to your immediate supervisor without delay

6. If a supervisor of a duplicating section in an agency hears a rumor concerning a change in agency personnel policy through the "grapevine," he should 6.____
   A. *repeat* it to his subordinates so they will be informed
   B. *not repeat* it to his subordinates before he determines the facts because, as supervisor, his work may give it unwarranted authority
   C. *repeat* it to his subordinates so that they will like him for confiding in them
   D. *not repeat* it to his subordinates before he determines the facts because a duplicating section is not concerned with matters of policy

7. When teaching a new employee how to operate a machine, a supervisor should FIRST 7.____
   A. let the employee try to operate the machine by himself, since he can learn only by his mistakes
   B. explain the process to him with the use of diagrams before showing him the machine
   C. have him memorize the details of the operation from the manual
   D. explain and demonstrate the various steps in the process, making sure he understands each step

8. If a subordinate accuses you of always giving him the least desirable assignments, you should IMMEDIATELY 8.____
   A. tell him that it is not true and you do not want to hear any more about it
   B. try to get specific details from him, so that you can find out what his impressions are based on
   C. tell him that you distribute assignments in the fairest way possible and he must be mistaken
   D. ask him what current assignment he has that he does not like, and assign it to someone else

9. Suppose that the production of an operator under your supervision has been unsatisfactory and you have decided to have a talk with him about it.
   During the interview, it would be BEST for you to 9.____
   A. discuss only the subordinate's weak points so that he can overcome them
   B. discuss only the subordinate's strong points so that he will not become discouraged
   C. compare the subordinate's work with that of his co-workers so that he will know what is expected of him
   D. discuss both his weak and strong points so that he will get a view of his overall performance

10. Suppose that an operator under your supervision makes a mistake in color on a 2,000-page job and runs it on white paper instead of on blue paper.
    Of the following, your BEST course in these circumstances would be to point out the error to the operator and 10.____
    A. have the operator rerun the job immediately on blue paper
    B. send the job to the person who ordered it without comment
    C. send the job to the person who ordered it and tell him it could not be done on blue paper
    D. ask the person who ordered the job whether the white paper is acceptable

11. Assuming that all your subordinates have equal technical competence, the BEST policy for a supervisor to follow when making assignments of undesirable jobs would be to 11.____
  A. distribute them as evenly as possible among his subordinates
  B. give them to the subordinate with the poorest attendance record
  C. ask the subordinate with the least seniority to do them
  D. assign them to the subordinate who is least likely to complain

12. To get the BEST results when training a number of subordinates at the same time, a supervisor should 12.____
  A. treat all of them in an identical manner to avoid accusations of favoritism
  B. treat them all fairly, but use different approaches in dealing with people of different personality types
  C. train only one subordinate, and have him train the others, because this will save a lot of the supervisor's time
  D. train first the subordinates who learn quickly so as to make the others think that the operation is easy to learn

13. Assume that, after a week's vacation, you return to find that one of your subordinates has produced a job which is unsatisfactory. 13.____
Your BEST course of action at that time would be to
  A. talk to your personnel department about implementing disciplinary action
  B. discuss unsatisfactory work in the unit at a meeting with all of your subordinates
  C. discuss the job with the subordinate to determine why he was unable to do it properly
  D. ignore the matter, because it is too late to correct the mistake

14. Suppose that an operator under your supervision informs you that Mr. Y, a senior administrator in your agency, has been submitting for copying many papers which are obviously personal in nature. The operator wants to know what to do about it, since the duplication of personal papers is against agency rules. 14.____
Your BEST course of action in these circumstances would be to
  A. tell the operator to pretend not to notice the content of the material and continue to copy whatever is given to him
  B. tell the operator that Mr. Y, as a senior administrator, must have gotten special permission to have personal papers duplicated
  C. have the operator refer Mr. Y to you and inform Mr. Y yourself that duplication of personal papers is against agency rules
  D. call Mr. Y's superior and tell him that Mr. Y has been having personal papers duplicated, which is against agency rules

15. Assume that you are teaching a certain process to an operator under your supervision. 15.____
In order to BEST determine whether he is actually learning what you are teaching, you should ask questions which
  A. can easily be answered by a "yes" or "no"
  B. require or encourage guessing

C. require a short description of what has been taught
D. are somewhat ambiguous so as to make the learner think about the procedures in question

16. If an employee is chronically late or absent, as his supervisor, it would be BEST for you to 16.____
A. let his work pile up so he can see that no one else will do it for him
B. discuss the matter with him and stress the importance of finding a solution
C. threaten to enter a written report on the matter into his personnel file
D. work out a system with him so he can have a different work schedule than the other employees

17. Assume that you have a subordinate who has just finished a basic training course in the operation of a machine. 17.____
Giving him a large and difficult FIRST assignment would be
A. *good*, because it would force him to "learn the ropes"
B. *bad*, because he would probably have difficulty in carrying it out, discouraging him and resulting in a waste of time and supplies
C. *good*, because how he handles it would give you an excellent basis for judging his competence
D. *bad*, because he would probably assume that you are discriminating against him

18. After putting a new employee under your supervision through an initial training period, assigning him to work with a more experienced employee for a while would be a 18.____
A. *good* idea, because it would give him the opportunity to observe what he had been taught and to participate in production himself
B. *bad* idea, because he should not be required to work under the direction of anyone who is not his supervisor
C. *good* idea, because it would raise the morale of the more experienced employee who could use him to do all the unpleasant chores
D. *bad* idea, because the best way for him to learn would be to give him full responsibility for assignments right away

19. Assume that a supervisor is responsible for ordering supplies for the duplicating section in his agency. 19.____
Which one of the following actions would be MOST helpful in determining when to place orders so that an adequate supply of materials will be on hand at all times?
A. Taking an inventory of supplies on hand at least every two months
B. Asking his subordinates to inform him when they see that supplies are low
C. Checking the inventory of supplies whenever he has time
D. Keeping a running inventory of supplies and a record of estimated needs

20. Routine procedures that have worked well in the past should be reviewed periodically by a supervisor MAINLY because 20.____
    A. they may have become outdated or in need of revision
    B. employees might dislike the procedures even though they have proven successful in the past
    C. these reviews are the main part of a supervisor's job
    D. this practice serves to give the supervisor an idea of how productive his subordinates are

21. Assume that an employee tells his supervisor about a grievance he has against a co-worker. The supervisor assures the employee that he will immediately take action to eliminate the grievance. 21.____
    The supervisor's attitude should be considered
    A. *correct*, because a good supervisor is one who can come to a quick decision
    B. *incorrect*, because the supervisor should have told the employee that he will investigate the grievance and then determine a future course of action
    C. *correct*, because the employee's morale will be higher, resulting in greater productivity
    D. *incorrect*, because the supervisor should remain uninvolved and let the employees settle grievances between themselves

22. If an employee's work output is low and of poor quality due to faulty work habits, the MOST constructive of the following ways for a supervisor to correct this situation generally is to 22.____
    A. discipline the employee
    B. transfer the employee to another unit
    C. provide additional training
    D. check the employee's work continuously

23. Assume that it becomes necessary for a supervisor to ask his staff to work overtime. 23.____
    Which one of the following techniques is MOST likely to win their willing cooperation to do this?
    A. Explain that this is part of their job specification entitled, "performs related work"
    B. Explain the reason it is necessary for the employees to work overtime
    C. Promise the employees special consideration regarding future leave matters
    D. Explain that if the employees do not work overtime, they will face possible disciplinary action

24. If an employee's work performance has recently fallen below established minimum standards for quality and quantity, the threat of demotion or other disciplinary measures as an attempt to improve this employee's performance would probably be the MOST acceptable and effective course of action 24.____
    A. *only* after other more constructive measures have failed
    B. *if* applied uniformly to all employees as soon as performance falls below standard

25. If, as a supervisor, it becomes necessary for you to assign an employee to supervise your unit during your vacation, it would generally be BEST to select the employee who 25.____
    A. is the best technician on the staff
    B. can get the work out smoothly, without friction
    C. has the most seniority
    D. is the most popular with the group

KEY (CORRECT ANSWERS)

1.	D	11.	A
2.	D	12.	B
3.	D	13.	C
4.	A	14.	C
5.	A	15.	C
6.	B	16.	B
7.	D	17.	B
8.	B	18.	A
9.	D	19.	D
10.	D	20.	A

21.	B
22.	C
23.	B
24.	A
25.	B

TEST 3

DIRECTIONS: Each question or incomplete statement is followed by several suggested answers or completions. Select the one that BEST answers the question or completes the statement. *PRINT THE LETTER OF THE CORRECT ANSWER IN THE SPACE AT THE RIGHT.*

1. An employee under your supervision has demonstrated a deep-seated personality problem that has begun to affect his work. 1.____
This situation should be
   A. *ignored*, mainly because such problems usually resolve themselves
   B. *handled*, mainly because the employee should be assisted in seeking professional help
   C. *ignored*, mainly because the employee will consider any advice as interference
   D. *handled*, mainly because the supervisors should be qualified to resolve deep-seated personality problems

2. Of the following, a supervisor will usually be MOST successful in maintaining employee morale while providing effective leadership if he 2.____
   A. takes prompt disciplinary action every time it is needed
   B. gives difficult assignments only to those workers who ask for such work
   C. promises his workers anything reasonable they request
   D. relies entirely on his staff for decisions

3. When a supervisor makes an assignment to his subordinates, he should include a clear statement of what results are expected when the assignment is completed. 3.____
Of the following, the BEST reason for following this procedure is that it will
   A. make it unnecessary for the supervisor to check on the progress of the work
   B. stimulate initiative and cooperation on the part of the more responsible workers
   C. give the subordinates a way to judge whether their work is meeting the requirements
   D. give the subordinates the feeling that they have some freedom of action

4. Assume that, on a new employee's first day of work, his supervisor gives him a good orientation by telling him the general regulations and procedures used in the office and introducing him to his department head and fellow employees. 4.____
For the remainder of the day, it would be BEST for the supervisor to
   A. give him steady instruction in all phases of his job, while stressing its most important aspects
   B. have him observe a fellow employee perform the duties of the job
   C. instruct him in that part of the job which he would prefer to learn first
   D. give him a simple task which requires little instruction and allows him to familiarize himself with the surroundings

5. When it becomes necessary to criticize subordinates because several errors in the unit's work have been discovered, the supervisor should USUALLY 5.____
   A. focus on the job operation and avoid placing personal blame
   B. make every effort to fix blame and admonish the person responsible
   C. include in the criticism those employees who recognize and rectify their own mistakes
   D. repeat the criticism at regular intervals in order to impress the subordinates with the seriousness of their errors

6. If two employees under your supervision are continually bickering and cannot get along together, the FIRST action that you should take is to 6.____
   A. investigate possible ways of separating them
   B. ask your immediate superior for the procedure to follow in this situation
   C. determine the cause of their difficulty
   D. develop a plan and tell both parties to try it

7. In general, it is appropriate to recommend the transfer of an employee for all of the following reasons EXCEPT 7.____
   A. rewarding him
   B. providing him with a more challenging job
   C. remedying an error in initial placement
   D. disciplining him

8. Of the following, the MAIN disadvantage of basing a training and development program on a series of lectures is that the lecture technique 8.____
   A. does not sufficiently involve trainees in the learning process
   B. is more costly than other methods of training
   C. cannot be used to facilitate the understanding of difficult information
   D. is time consuming and inefficient

9. A supervisor has been assigned to train a new employee who is properly motivated but has made many mistakes. 9.____
   In the interview between the supervisor and employee about this problem, the employee should FIRST be
   A. asked if he can think of anything that he can do to improve his work
   B. complimented sincerely on some aspect of his work that is satisfactory
   C. asked to explain why he made the mistake
   D. advised that he may be dismissed if he continues to be careless

10. In training subordinates for more complex work, a supervisor must be aware of the progress that the subordinates are making. 10.____
   Determination of the results that have been accomplished by training is a concept commonly known as
   A. reinforcement B. feedback
   C. cognitive dissonance D. the halo effect

11. Assume that one of your subordinates loses interest in his work because he feels that your recent evaluation of his performance was unfair. 11.____
The one of the following which is the BEST way to help him is to
A. establish frequent deadlines for his work
B. discuss his feelings and attitude with him
C. discuss with him only the positive aspects of his performance
D. arrange for his transfer to another unit

12. Informal organizations often develop at work. 12.____
Of the following, the supervisor should realize that these groups will USUALLY
A. determine work pace through unofficial agreements
B. restrict vital communication channels
C. lower morale by providing a chance to spread grievances
D. provide leaders who will substitute for the supervisor when he is absent

13. Assume that you, the supervisor, have called to your office a subordinate whom, on several recent occasions, you have seen using the office telephone for personal use. 13.____
In this situation, it would be MOST appropriate to begin the interview by
A. discussing the disciplinary action that you believe to be warranted
B. asking the subordinate to explain the reason for his personal use of the office telephone
C. telling the subordinate about other employees who were disciplined for the same offense
D. informing the subordinate that he is not to use the office telephone under any circumstances until further notice

14. Of the following, the success of any formal training program depends PRIMARILY upon the 14.____
A. efficient and thorough preparation of materials, facilities, and procedures for instruction
B. training program's practical relevance to the on-the-job situation
C. scheduling of training sessions so as to minimize interference with normal job responsibilities
D. creation of a positive initial reception on the part of the trainees

15. All of the following are legitimate purposes for regularly evaluating employee performance EXCEPT 15.____
A. stimulating improvement in performance
B. developing more accurate standards to be used in future ratings
C. encouraging a spirit of competition
D. allowing the employee to set realistic work goals for himself

16. A certain supervisor is very conscientious. He wants to receive personally all reports, correspondence, etc., and to be completely involved in all of the unit's operations. However, he is having difficulty in keeping up with the growing amount of paperwork. 16.____

Of the following, the MOST desirable course of action for him to take is to
A. put in more hours on the job
B. ask for additional office help
C. begin to delegate more of his work
D. inquire of his supervisor if the paperwork is really necessary

17. Assume that you are a supervisor. One of the workers under your supervision expresses his need to speak to you about a client who has been particularly uncooperative in providing information. 17.____
The MOST appropriate action for you to take FIRST would be to
A. agree to see the client for the worker in order to get the information
B. advise the worker to try several more times to get the information before he asks you for help
C. tell the worker you will go with him to see the client in order to observe his technique
D. ask the worker some questions in order to determine the type of help he needs in the situation

18. The supervisor who is MOST likely to achieve a high level of productivity from the professional employees under his supervision is the one who 18.____
A. watches their progress continuously
B. provides them with just enough information to carry out their assigned tasks
C. occasionally pitches in and helps them with their work
D. shares with them responsibility for setting work goals

19. Assume that there has been considerable friction for some time among the workers of a certain unit. The supervisor in charge of this unit becomes aware that the problem is getting serious as shown by increased absenteeism and lateness, loud arguments, etc. 19.____
Of the following, the BEST course of action for the supervisor to take FIRST is to
A. have a staff discussion about objectives and problems
B. seek out and penalize the apparent trouble-makers
C. set up and enforce stricter formal rules
D. discipline the next subordinate who causes friction

20. Assume that an employee under your supervision asks you for some blank paper and pencils to take home to her young grandson who, she says, delights in drawing. 20.____
The one of the following actions you SHOULD take is to
A. give her the material she wants and refrain from any comment
B. refuse her request and tell her that the use of office supplies for personal reasons is not proper
C. give her the material but suggest that she buy it next time
D. tell her to take the material herself since you do not want to know anything about the matter

21. A certain supervisor is given a performance evaluation by his superior. In it he is commended for his method of "delegation," a term that USUALLY refers to the action of 21.____
    A. determining the priorities for activities which must be completed
    B. assigning to subordinates some of the duties for which he is responsible
    C. standardizing operations in order to achieve results as close as possible to established goals
    D. dividing the activities necessary to achieve an objective into simple steps

22. A supervisor is approached by a subordinate who complains that a fellow worker is not assuming his share of the workload and is, therefore, causing more work for others in the office. 22.____
    Of the following, the MOST appropriate action for the supervisor to take in response to this complaint is to tell the subordinate
    A. that he will look into the matter
    B. to concentrate on his own job and not to worry about others
    C. to discuss the matter with the other worker
    D. that not everyone is capable of working at the same pace

23. Aside from the formal relationships established by management, informal and unofficial relationships will be developed among the personnel within an organization. 23.____
    Of the following, the MAIN importance of such informal relationships to the operations of the formal organization is that they
    A. reinforce the basic goals of the formal organization
    B. insure the interchangeability of the personnel within the organization
    C. provide an additional channel of communications within the organization
    D. insure predictability and control of the behavior of members of the organization

24. The most productive worker in a unit frequently takes overly-long coffee breaks and lunch hours while maintaining his above-average rate of productivity. 24.____
    Of the following, it would be MOST advisable for the supervisor to
    A. reprimand him, because rules must be enforced equally regardless of the merit of an individual's job performance
    B. ignore the infractions because a superior worker should be granted extra privileges for his efforts
    C. take no action unless others in the unit complain, because a reprimand may hurt the superior worker's feelings and cause him to produce less
    D. tell other members of the unit that a comparable rate of productivity on their part will be rewarded with similar privileges

25. A supervisor has been asked by his superior to choose an employee to supervise a special project. 25.____
Of the following, the MOST significant factor to consider in making this choice is the employee's
   A. length of service
   B. ability to do the job
   C. commitment to the goals of the agency
   D. attitude toward his fellow workers

KEY (CORRECT ANSWERS)

1.	B	11.	B
2.	A	12.	A
3.	C	13.	B
4.	D	14.	B
5.	A	15.	C
6.	C	16.	C
7.	D	17.	D
8.	A	18.	D
9.	B	19.	A
10.	B	20.	B

21.	B
22.	A
23.	C
24.	A
25.	B

TEST 4

DIRECTIONS: Each question or incomplete statement is followed by several suggested answers or completions. Select the one that BEST answers the question or completes the statement. *PRINT THE LETTER OF THE CORRECT ANSWER IN THE SPACE AT THE RIGHT.*

1. Assume that you are a newly appointed supervisor. Your MOST important responsibility is to 1.____
   A. make certain that all of the employees under your supervision are treated equally
   B. reduce disciplinary situations to a minimum
   C. insure an atmosphere of mutual trust between your workers and yourself
   D. see that the required work is done properly

2. In order to make sure that work is completed on time, the supervisor should 2.____
   A. pitch in and do as much of the work herself as she can
   B. schedule the work and control its progress
   C. not assign more than one person to any one task
   D. assign the same amount of work to each subordinate

3. Assume that you are a supervisor in charge of a number of workers who do the same kind of work and who each produce about the same volume of work in a given period of time. When their performance is evaluated, the worker who should be rated as the MOST accurate is the one 3.____
   A. whose errors are the easiest to correct
   B. whose errors involve the smallest amount of money
   C. who makes the fewest errors in her work
   D. who makes fewer errors as she becomes more experienced

4. As a supervisor, you have been asked by the manager to recommend whether the work of the bookkeeping office requires a permanent increase in bookkeeping office staff. Of the following questions, the one whose answer would be MOST likely to assist you in making your recommendation is: 4.____
   A. Are temporary employees hired to handle seasonal fluctuations in work loads?
   B. Are some permanent employees working irregular hours because they occasionally work overtime?
   C. Are the present permanent employees keeping the work of the bookkeeping office current?
   D. Are employees complaining that the work is unevenly divided?

5. Assume that you are a supervisor. One of your subordinates tells you that he is dissatisfied with his work assignment and that he wishes to discuss the matter with you. The employee is obviously very angry and upset. Of the following, the course of action that you should take FIRST in this situation is to 5.____
   A. promise the employee that you will review all the work assignments in the office to determine whether any changes should be made.
   B. have the employee present his complaint, correcting him whenever he makes what seems to be an erroneous charge against you
   C. postpone discussion of the employee's complaint, explaining to him that the matter can be settled more satisfactory if it is discussed calmly
   D. permit the employee to present his complaint in full, withholding your comments until he has finished making his complaint

6. Assume that you are a supervisor. You find that you are spending too much time on routine tasks and not enough time on supervision of the work of your subordinates. It would be ADVISABLE for you to 6.____
   A. assign some of the routine tasks to your subordinates
   B. postpone the performance of routine tasks until you have completed your supervisory tasks
   C. delegate the supervisory work to a capable subordinate
   D. eliminate some of the supervisory tasks that you are required to perform

7. Assume that you are a supervisor. You discover that one of your workers has violated an important rule. The FIRST course of action for you as the supervisor to take would be to 7.____
   A. call a meeting of the entire staff and discuss the matter generally without mentioning any employee by name
   B. arrange to supervise the offending worker's activities more closely
   C. discuss the violation privately with the worker involved
   D. discuss the matter with the worker within hearing of the entire staff so that she will feel too ashamed to commit this violation in the future

8. As a supervisor, you are to prepare a vacation schedule for the bookkeeping office employees. The one of the following that is the LEAST important factor for you to consider in setting up this schedule is 8.____
   A. seniority
   B. vacation preferences of employees
   C. average productivity of the office

9. In assigning a complicated task to a group of subordinates, a certain supervisor does not indicate the specific steps to be followed in performing the assignment, nor does he designate which subordinate is to be responsible for seeing that the task is done on time. 9.____

This supervisor's method of assigning the task is MOST likely to result in
A. confusion among subordinates with consequent delays in work
B. greater individual effort and self-reliance
C. assumption of authority by capable subordinates
D. loss of confidence by subordinates in their ability

10. While you are explaining a new procedure to an employee, she asks you a question about the procedure which you cannot answer. 10.____
The MOST appropriate action for you to take is to
A. admit your inability to answer the question and promise to obtain the information
B. point out the likelihood of a situation arising which would require an answer to the question
C. ask the worker to give her reason for asking the question before you give any further reply
D. tell her to inform you immediately should a situation arise requiring an answer to her question

KEY (CORRECT ANSWERS)

1.	D	6.	A
2.	B	7.	C
3.	C	8.	C
4.	C	9.	A
5.	D	10.	A

SUPERVISION, ADMINISTRATION, MANAGEMENT AND ORGANIZATION

EXAMINATION SECTION

TEST 1

DIRECTIONS: Each question or incomplete statement is followed by several suggested answers or completions. Select the one that BEST answers the question or completes the statement. *PRINT THE LETTER OF THE CORRECT ANSWER IN THE SPACE AT THE RIGHT.*

1. A foreman finds it necessary to discipline two of his laborers. One man had been smoking near the gasoline pump and another man had come to work late four days in a row. 1.____
Which of the following actions by the foreman would be MOST appropriate?
   A. Before taking "disciplinary action," speak to both men together so they can see how much each other's difficulties are related and learn how to avoid repeating both kinds of bad practices.
   B. Before taking "disciplinary action," speak to each man privately since each has been involved in a different problem and each should get the foreman's full attention.
   C. Warn the man who was smoking near the gas pump but recommend dismissal for the habitual latecomer.
   D. Recommend suspension for the man who was careless enough to smoke near the gas pump and warn the other man.

2. Suppose that you are supervising an important field project and your own supervisor calls you back to the office to discuss a scheduling problem. You know that you will be away from your crew for more than an hour. 2.____
Which of the following would be the BEST action to insure that the project continues as it should?
   A. Tell your crew that you will be gone and that you expect them to work just as they do while you are with them.
   B. Put an experienced and reliable member of your crew in charge while you are gone; and tell the crew he is in charge until you get back.
   C. Leave after making sure the men are working steadily; to place one man in charge, above the rest, would destroy morale.
   D. Ask a trusted member of your crew to say nothing, but to observe the rest of the crew and report to you later.

3. A foreman received a memo from central office describing a new but somewhat complicated work method to be used by his men. He didn't talk to his men about the new method because he knew that they had received copies of the same memo. 3.____

For this supervisor to have acted in this way was a
A. *good* idea, because time was saved by not discussing something already known by his men
B. *good* idea, because discussing the new method might have stimulated objections from his men
C. *bad* idea, mainly because he should have made sure his men understood the new method
D. *bad* idea, mainly because the foreman should have asked his men their opinion on the new procedure

4. An experienced supervisor teaching new workers often overlooks so-called minor points because of his great familiarity with the job. When an instructor takes such points for granted, he leaves gaps in his instruction. 4.____
Of the following, the BEST way to help prevent this kind of oversight is to
A. teach each new worker individually
B. ask the new workers if they have any questions after the explanation and demonstration
C. teach the new workers in a group
D. break down the operation into simple parts when planning the lesson

5. Suppose that you have just been appointed as foreman. You feel that because one of the members of your crew is older than you, he may resent your authority. 5.____
Of the following, the BEST way to handle this situation is to
A. give him tougher assignments at first to bring him in line
B. in the presence of the rest of the crew ask him, whenever possible, for suggestions on how to improve the work
C. give him the easier assignments so that he won't resent taking orders from you
D. treat him as a member of the crew who must receive your leadership and guidance

6. Right after you, a foreman, have trained a worker to do a new but uncomplicated job, you find that, although he is doing it correctly, it will take him four or five hours to finish, and you have several other groups of men in the area upon whom you would like to check. 6.____
What is the BEST way to handle this situation?
A. Check on the other men but visit the new man a few times until he finishes the job to make sure he continues to do it correctly
B. Stay with the new man until he is finished, to keep him from losing confidence in himself
C. Check out the new man every half hour or so and ask him questions to make sure he hasn't forgotten anything
D. Stay away from the new man until he is finished in order to show that you have confidence in him, but check on the other men

7. A foreman has just received a new piece of equipment never used by his crew before. His expectation is that he will have to train anyone who uses the equipment. However, the man he is about to assign tells the foreman that he has worked with such equipment before. The foreman, somewhat surprised, asks the laborer what he knows about using the equipment. 7.____
This action is
   A. *good*; the information may help the foreman in instructing the laborer
   B. *poor*; it simply increases the time needed, since the foreman's responsibility to instruct the laborer still remains
   C. *good*; the laborer may suggest improvements in the equipment
   D. *poor*; the laborer probably would not know much about the new equipment

8. One of the men under your supervision suggests a new procedure for keeping control of tools and materials loaded on trucks. You consider this method better than the old one which you felt needed improvement. 8.____
Which of the following is the BEST thing to do?
   A. Ignore the idea; when a worker has too many of his suggestions accepted, he begins to feel too big to accept supervision
   B. Try out the new method, telling your men where the idea came from, and ask if they have any additional ideas
   C. Institute the method with no comment to the men, but recommend a bonus for the man who suggested the idea
   D. Institute the new method, explaining that this change has been considered by yourself and management for a long time

9. Suppose it is permissible for a new kind of power tool to be used by several workers under your supervision and you are responsible for teaching them how to use the tool. 9.____
Which of the following approaches is the BEST one to take?
   A. Get them together, let them ask questions on the tool, then proceed on the basis of their questions
   B. Give them a talk on how to operate this tool and explain everything before permitting any questions
   C. Demonstrate and explain the operation of the tool and then let each worker operate the machine while you and the others watch
   D. Give each worker a set of instructions to read first and ask them questions about what they have read, before you actually teach them

10. An employee complains to you, the foreman, that he is getting more unpleasant jobs than anyone else in the crew. When you later review your assignments, you find that, inadvertently, you have tended to give this man the more difficult and unpleasant jobs, perhaps because he is such a good worker. 10.____
What is the BEST way to handle this situation?
   A. Tell the employee that you will see to it that he does not get any more unpleasant jobs
   B. Do not discuss it with him, but give him fairer assignments in the future

C. Tell the employee your findings and that you will see to it that he is not treated unfairly in the future
D. Tell the employee that the reason he gets the more difficult jobs is that he is a good worker

11. A foreman immediately spoke to a laborer about a mistake the laborer made and then the man never made that particular mistake again; but the foreman reminded the man about the mistake whenever he saw him working at the kind of job on which the mistake had been made. 11.____
This action of reminding the man was
A. *good*, because this constant reminder helps the laborer to avoid repeating his mistake
B. *bad*, because it is unnecessary to remind the laborer of mistakes he is no longer likely to make
C. *good*, because this shows the worker that the foreman has a good memory and is not likely to miss any other mistakes
D. *bad*, because it is very likely that the foreman may embarrass the man by mentioning the mistake in front of other workers

12. Sometimes it is necessary to give out written orders or to post written or typed information on a bulletin board rather than to merely give spoken orders. The foreman must decide how he will do it. 12.____
In which of the following situations would it be BETTER for him to give written rather than spoken orders?
A. He is going to reassign a man from one work crew to another crew under his supervision in the same borough.
B. His men must be informed of a permanent change in a complicated operating procedure.
C. A man must be transferred from acting as regular helper on a truck to working with a plumber's gang.
D. He must order a group of men to do a difficult and dirty job to which most of them are likely to object.

13. Suppose your supervisor tells you that your crew takes too long doing snow removal operations because they are not following correct procedures. When he reviews the procedures with you, you suddenly realize that you had trained the men incorrectly. 13.____
Of the following, the BEST thing for you to do now is to
A. teach your men the correct method with no explanation
B. tell your men that your superior has just decided to change the method
C. tell your men that you want them to try another method to see if the job can be done more quickly
D. tell your men you gave them the wrong information and that you have to correct it

14. Building morale is one of the greatest responsibilities of any superior. A basic factor in good morale is the degree of interest subordinates have in their work. 14.____
Which one of the following is the BEST way for a supervisor to develop interest in the job among his employees?

A. Review all work done by your employees to be sure it is correct
B. Criticize work which is well done to make sure it is better the next time
C. Show your approval to your employees when they do a good job
D. Show your interest in your employees' personal life

15. The supervisor represents management in instructing his subordinates in safe working practices and in seeing to it that workers follow these practices. 15.____
Which if the following can be MOST reasonably concluded from this statement?
A. From management's viewpoint, the supervisor is responsible for controlling accidents in his area of supervision.
B. Management has primary responsibility for setting up policies for the supervisor on safe working practices.
C. All accidents must be immediately reported to management by the supervisor.
D. Supervisors cannot be held responsible if an employee willfully ignores safe working practices.

16. Of the following, the MOST important thing to do when you assign work to men is to give 16.____
A. the most unpleasant jobs to men who are least likely to complain
B. the best jobs to the best workers
C. each man work according to his ability
D. each man work according to his seniority

17. Proper training is an important part of any job. 17.____
Which of the following is NOT considered a result of effective training?
A. Increased need to hire new workers
B. Reduced waste of time and materials
C. Increased quality of production
D. Improved employee morale

18. For a foreman to be directly involved in the instruction and training of his men in work methods and use of basic tools and implements is 18.____
A. *inadvisable*, mainly because workers will have many opportunities to learn from more experienced workers during the course of their daily work
B. *advisable*, mainly because it is the foreman's responsibility to see to it that his men know and do their jobs
C. *inadvisable*, mainly because other more important subjects constantly require the attention of a foreman
D. *advisable*, mainly because training methods are changing constantly and the foreman should keep up with them

19. When a foreman assigns A and B to do a certain job, they usually finish it adequately in 1½ hours. When he assigns C and D to do the same job, they usually take 2 hours to finish it adequately. 19.____

Of the following, the MOST reasonable conclusion that the foreman can draw from this wide difference is that

A. he can expect A and B to be faster than C and D on most jobs
B. this job is not the kind which should be judged by the time taken to do it
C. C and D do not like this particular job as much as other jobs
D. C and D may need additional training to do this job faster

20. You, a foreman, tell your supervisor that you need some new equipment and he asks you to write him a note to which he can refer when forwarding your request. 20.____
Of the following, the MOST important thing to include in your request is

A. your estimate of how long it would take to get delivery of the new equipment after it is ordered
B. an explanation of why the new equipment is needed
C. the names of the laborers who would use the new equipment
D. the length of time you think the new equipment will last

21. When one of the laborers had an accident while using a defective drill machine, the foreman began writing an accident report as soon as he finished giving first aid and had referred the man for treatment. 21.____
This *immediate* writing of the report was

A. *inadvisable*; he should have let more time go by to collect his thoughts
B. *good*; the chance of forgetting important facts about the accident was reduced
C. *inadvisable*; other employees might think that the foreman was eager to cover up the circumstances of the accident
D. *good*; primarily because such action permits the statistics in the department to be kept right up to date

22. The MOST important objective of the foreman's investigating every accident on the job is to 22.____

A. determine who was responsible for the accident
B. eliminate the conditions or actions which have caused accidents
C. gather information for the department's legal defense
D. decide how the person responsible for the accident should be disciplined

23. A man cuts his leg with a shovel he was using to dig a hole. He is on the ground and bleeding. A number of your men are around him, helping and encouraging him to keep his spirits up. 23.____
Of the following, the FIRST thing you should do in this situation is to

A. find out how the accident occurred, since the men are already helping him
B. get the facts for the accident report while the men give him first aid
C. keep too many men from crowding around the injured man and give him the necessary first aid
D. apply a tourniquet and get him on a truck to a hospital

24. As a foreman, you see a laborer carrying a small electrical appliance by its service cord and you tell him not to carry it that way. 24.____
Of the following, the MAIN reason why the laborer should not carry the appliance by the cord is that
   A. the appliance may be damaged if it strikes against a solid object
   B. he may get a shock from the current that remains in the unplugged cord
   C. the appliance might strike against him or others, causing injury
   D. the cord might be damaged or broken

25. A fire breaks out in electrical equipment. As a foreman, you see a laborer pull an emergency fire hose and direct a stream of water into the equipment to put the fire out. 25.____
The laborer's action was
   A. *good*; water is the most effective extinguishing agent to use on electrical fires
   B. *bad*; this is a dangerous action since wet material often can conduct electricity
   C. *good*; water is the only extinguishing agent that will not damage the insulation
   D. *bad*; while no additional danger was created, water will not put out electrical fires

KEY (CORRECT ANSWERS)

1.	B	11.	B
2.	B	12.	B
3.	C	13.	D
4.	D	14.	C
5.	D	15.	A
6.	A	16.	C
7.	A	17.	A
8.	B	18.	B
9.	C	19.	D
10.	C	20.	B

21.	B
22.	B
23.	C
24.	D
25.	B

TEST 2

DIRECTIONS: Each question or incomplete statement is followed by several suggested answers or completions. Select the one that BEST answers the question or completes the statement. *PRINT THE LETTER OF THE CORRECT ANSWER IN THE SPACE AT THE RIGHT.*

1. When changes which the men might not like are made in construction methods, a *good* foreman should 1.____
   A. tell the men to adopt the new methods and not to bother him with questions
   B. assign a senior man in his crew to instruct the men in the new methods and tell the senior man that he has full responsibility for the instructions
   C. explain to the men that he does not like the new methods, but that it was not his decision to make
   D. explain to the men, as far as possible, all the reasons for adopting the new methods

2. When a citizen complains to a foreman that the equipment on a job under his supervision is causing too much noise, the foreman should 2.____
   A. tell the citizen that the project will soon be finished
   B. investigate the complaint to see if it is valid
   C. stop all work immediately
   D. ignore the complaint

3. Participation of foremen in employee safety training programs as instructors should be 3.____
   A. *encouraged*, since it is a means of enhancing motivation
   B. *discouraged*, since it is poor policy to let the men see the foreman work
   C. *discouraged*, since it wastes the foremen's time
   D. *required*, since the foremen are the only ones qualified to instruct

4. When training a group of trainees, the foreman should 4.____
   A. set up a rigid program assuming that all trainees have the same skills
   B. eliminate any trainee who does not demonstrate aptitude in all types of work
   C. adjust the program to account for individual differences in trainees
   D. eliminate any topics which the trainees do not want

5. If a new man in a foreman's crew feels that he cannot perform a specific task, the foreman should 5.____
   A. transfer the new man to another crew
   B. give the new man the necessary training to do it
   C. tell the new man he has to learn, on his own time, to do the task
   D. tell the new man he is expected to do the task as best as he can

6. The encoding encouragement by a foreman of competition between trainees in a training program is 6.____
   A. *inadvisable*, because some trainees perform better than others
   B. *advisable*, because it provides an incentive to the trainees
   C. *inadvisable*, because they are all paid at the same rate
   D. *advisable*, because the foreman will have more free time

7. It is necessary to shut off the water in a main temporarily in order to make repairs. 7.____
   In order for the foreman to get cooperation from the general public, the
   A. job should be done at night so that few people will be aware of it
   B. shut-off crew should be ordered not to speak to the general public
   C. job should be done in several stages so that the public realizes how difficult the problem is
   D. purpose and duration of the shut-off should be explained to the general public

8. Of the following, the one which a foreman should NOT do if he wants the willing cooperation of his men is 8.____
   A. do everything in his power to provide his men with adequate equipment
   B. praise his men after they do an exceptional job
   C. use authority sparingly
   D. show favoritism to the men who do not complain about the work

9. When a new employee joins a foreman's crew, the foreman should 9.____
   A. guide the new employee through the adjustment period in a friendly, sympathetic manner
   B. speak to the new employee as little as possible
   C. avoid the new employee completely
   D. give the new employee no responsibility

10. When a man with many years of service is transferred to a foreman's crew to perform a type of work at which he is inexperienced, the foreman should 10.____
   A. expect him to know the safety procedures for the new working conditions
   B. not embarrass the man by giving him safety instructions
   C. give him the same safety instructions a new employee gets
   D. assign him to work with the crew that had the latest accident to learn the safety procedures

11. Of the following, the one that is the BEST objective of an employee suggestion program is to 11.____
   A. create more jobs
   B. increase workload of each employee
   C. increase idle time between jobs
   D. stimulate employees' interest in their jobs

12. Of the following, the one that is NOT required in order to be an effective foreman is the ability to 12.____
    A. delegate all responsibilities
    B. use proper instructional methods
    C. build morale
    D. make a tentative decision

13. Of the following, the FIRST step to be taken by a foreman when he must make a decision in regard to a construction problem is to 13.____
    A. get all the facts
    B. decide
    C. evaluate the facts
    D. make a tentative decision

14. When an employee, who previously had a record of promptness, is frequently late, the BEST action for the foreman to take in order to correct the employee's lateness is to 14.____
    A. ignore the lateness because the employee will come in on time as soon as it is possible to do so
    B. recommend that he be discharged
    C. scold him in front of the rest of the men to set an example
    D. tell him that disciplinary action will be taken if he continues to be late

15. Of the following actions, the one that MOST probably NOT an indication that a subordinate has a potential grievance is that the subordinate 15.____
    A. very often becomes grouchy and irritable on the job
    B. goes to the washroom more often than usual to read a newspaper
    C. frequently comes to the foreman with minor suggestions
    D. is frequently late

16. In dealing with grievances, a foreman should 16.____
    A. do whatever is necessary to satisfy the employee
    B. realize that some persons make demands that cannot be met
    C. state the rules and regulations and not discuss the situation further
    D. wait until the situation changes before acting on the grievance

17. If a foreman detects low morale in his crew, he should FIRST 17.____
    A. investigate the causes and attempt to eliminate them
    B. tell top management so that they can find out what is wrong
    C. ignore it
    D. request that at least one-half of the crew be transferred

18. Of the following, the one that is NOT a proper procedure to follow in settling grievances is 18.____
    A. to settle grievances promptly
    B. to settle grievances on merit only
    C. for top management alone to settle grievances
    D. settle grievances on the basis of as many relevant acts as possible

19. A foreman is approached by a homeowner who asks the foreman to have his crew remove a large tree from his backyard and offers the foreman $25 for doing the work. 19.____

Of the following, the BEST action for the foreman to take is to
- A. order his crew to do the work and keep the money
- B. order the crew to do the work and divide the money among his crew
- C. politely refuse to do the work
- D. order his men to do the work and refuse to take any money

20. Of the following, the MOST important purpose of a good report made by a foreman is to 20.____
    - A. provide the information needed at the time and on the subject under consideration
    - B. justify the manpower expenditure in making the report
    - C. eliminate the necessity of each of his subordinates' making a report
    - D. prevent the public from blaming the department for its action

21. When the men under his supervision are not producing work of the desired quality, the foreman should FIRST 21.____
    - A. scold him
    - B. find out what is causing the defects
    - C. make sure that the men have a good reason for producing poor quality work
    - D. notify the district foreman

22. Under the normal daily working conditions, if Foreman X requests Foreman Y for the services of a laborer, Foreman Y should 22.____
    - A. send his most capable laborer
    - B. send his least capable laborer
    - C. ignore Foreman X
    - D. refer Foreman X to the supervising foreman

23. One of the steps a foreman should take in order to encourage subordinates to cooperate with him is to 23.____
    - A. see that tools and materials are available in the right quantity when needed
    - B. let his men participate in deciding all important decisions by taking a vote
    - C. let his men leave work early at least once a week
    - D. try to give him deadlines that are very difficult to meet

24. Of the following, the one which is NOT a requirement of a satisfactory report by a foreman is that it should be 24.____
    A. timely B. lengthy C. legible D. accurate

25. When an accident occurs, the FIRST concern of the foreman should be to 25.____
    - A. see that the injured person is properly cared for
    - B. make sketches of the area
    - C. interview the injured person
    - D. interview witnesses and co-workers

KEY (CORRECT ANSWERS)

1. D
2. B
3. A
4. C
5. B
6. B
7. D
8. D
9. A
10. C
11. D
12. A
13. A
14. D
15. C
16. B
17. A
18. C
19. C
20. A
21. B
22. D
23. A
24. B
25. A

TEST 3

DIRECTIONS: Each question or incomplete statement is followed by several suggested answers or completions. Select the one that BEST answers the question or completes the statement. *PRINT THE LETTER OF THE CORRECT ANSWER IN THE SPACE AT THE RIGHT.*

1. Of the following considerations, the one which is LEAST important is that every employee under your supervision 1.____
   A. knows how to do his job
   B. reports to you right after completing one activity, before starting another
   C. knows exactly what his specific duties are
   D. has the desire to fulfill his job responsibilities

2. Of the following, the MOST important part of your job as a foreman is to see that 2.____
   A. your superior is satisfied
   B. the morale of your subordinates is high
   C. the work is done satisfactorily
   D. absenteeism and lateness are kept to a minimum

3. The one of the following which is the MOST valid reason for setting a time limit on a particular job is 3.____
   A. to insure that the work will be of the best quality
   B. that this is the only way of getting maximum output
   C. that this particular job must be completed within a specified time limit
   D. to keep the men continuously busy

4. The need for disciplining can BEST be reduced if the foreman 4.____
   A. posts a list of rules
   B. is a stern task master
   C. is on friendly terms with all the subordinates
   D. gives subordinates the best possible supervision

5. Of the following actions, the one MOST likely to weaken the authority of a foreman in the eyes of his men is: 5.____
   A. Reviewing periodically the accepted standards of work and conduct
   B. Consulting with his boss on all matters which are of a routine nature
   C. Posting a minimum number of rules
   D. Listening willingly to suggestions from any of his men

6. Assume that, as a foreman, you are informed by your boss that one of your new men has complained about the way you handle your crew. Since this man has never come to you with any complaints, you should FIRST 6.____
   A. tell the rest of the crew that he has been carrying tales
   B. think over your handling of this man and consider whether any action of yours might have discouraged him from speaking to you
   C. bawl the man out for going over your head
   D. tell the man in private that you will keep a close watch on him in the future

7. Before recommending that charges be preferred against one of his men for breaking the rules, the foreman should FIRST make sure that 7.____
   A. his superior will approve the recommendation
   B. the charges will be sustained at the hearing
   C. he has all the necessary information on the case
   D. the man's fellow workers will give testimony favorable to the foreman's side of the case

8. A foreman hears a loud argument going on between two of his men. 8.____
   Of the following actions, the one the foreman should take FIRST is to
   A. take the men to his boss so that the matter can be settled
   B. send one of the men involved in the argument to another job
   C. find out the cause of the argument
   D. ask one of the other men what he thinks is the cause of the argument

9. Assume that a foreman's supervisor has discovered a mistake in one of the jobs done by the foreman's crew. 9.____
   The BEST action for the foreman to take is to
   A. find out which of his men made the mistake and see to it that the man is not given similar work again
   B. tell the supervisor which one of his men made the mistake
   C. explain that the mistake was probably made because the foreman had so many new men
   D. accept responsibility for the mistake and correct it

10. Assume that you, a foreman, are told by another foreman that one of your men violated a safety rule. 10.____
   Of the following, the BEST action for you to take is to
   A. tell the other foreman to leave your men alone
   B. speak to the man about the incident
   C. give your entire gang a strong talk on safety procedures citing the incident as a reason
   D. watch this man closely in order to catch him next time

11. Of the following courses of action, the FIRST one that a foreman should take if one of his men violates a minor safety rule is to 11.____
   A. explain to the man how small mistakes can cause serious accidents
   B. request that the rest of the gang keep an eye on the man
   C. tell the man that everyone makes small mistakes and not to get upset about it
   D. point out to the man that the only way he will learn is by making mistakes

12. Employees, generally, do not object to strict rules and regulations if the rules 12.____
   A. result in greater understanding of the job
   B. are enforced without bias or favor
   C. deal with routine phases of the work
   D. affect the senior men more than the junior

13. The one of the following which is NOT a good practice in administering discipline is for the foreman to 13.____
    A. allow the employee to reply to his criticism if he wishes
    B. reprimand the employee in private even though the mistake occurred in the presence of others
    C. allow an extended period of time to elapse after an error has been discovered before reprimanding the employee
    D. be sure he has all the facts before he reprimands the employee

14. A foreman should realize that the performance of unpleasant duties is, generally, 14.____
    A. *undesirable* and should be avoided whenever possible
    B. *unavoidable* and is part of his responsibility as a leader
    C. *desirable*, because the self-discipline required insures supervisory growth
    D. *avoidable*, since there is always a way tom make a job pleasant

15. Some discussions between a worker and a foreman require privacy. 15.____
    Of the following, the one which LEAST requires discussion in private is
    A. reprimanding a worker for an error
    B. informing a worker that his leave has been approved
    C. listening to one worker's expressions of dissatisfaction with working conditions
    D. determining causes of frequent absenteeism

16. Assume that several of your men start a heated discussion during working hours about rumored changes in assignment. 16.____
    Of the following, the BEST way for the foreman to deal with this situation would be to break up the discussion and tell the men that
    A. he will check on the rumor
    B. the existing assignments are satisfactory
    C. the methods by which assignments are made do not concern them
    D. they should wait until new assignments, if any, are made, before complaining

17. A foreman is BEST qualified to investigate accidents involving his subordinates because he 17.____
    A. has all safety equipment for the job
    B. has more free time than his superiors
    C. has more skill than his superiors
    D. is familiar with all the job conditions

Questions 18-25.

DIRECTIONS: The following table shows the requests made by the staff for vacation. This table is to be used, along with the Rules and Guidelines, to make the decisions and judgments called for in each of Questions 18 through 25.

VACATION REQUESTS FOR THE ONE-YEAR PERIOD
MAY 1, 2023 THROUGH APRIL 30, 2024
Accumulated Annual Leave

Name	Title	Date Appointed	Days Through April 30, 2023	Requested Vacation Periods
Williams	Laborer	June 2007	31	Sept. 18-Oct. 6; Nov. 6-17
Ortiz	Laborer	Apr. 2019	23	July 24-Aug. 11; Oct. 16-20
Mullen	Laborer	Aug. 2008	36	June 26-Aug. 4; Nov. 6-10
Jones	Foreman	Sept. 2006	35	June 5-23; July 31-Sept. 1
Greenberg	Laborer	Dec. 2021	20	July 24-28; Feb. 5-23
Castoni	Laborer	Feb. 2019	28	May 22-June 2; June 28-July 7
Phillips	Laborer	May 2017	24	Mar. 19-Apr. 6; Apr. 23-May 4
Gilbert	Laborer	July 2013	32	June 19-July 14; Aug. 21-Sept. 1
Hart	Director	Jan. 2001	36	May 15-June 16; July 17-28
Reyes	Laborer	Aug. 2021	26	Oct. 2-27; Feb. 5-9
Spencer	Laborer	May 2008	33	May 22-June 9; Nov. 6-24
Clark	Laborer	Oct. 2017	29	June 5-9; Oct. 9-20

RULES AND GUIDELINES

1. For the period Jun 1 through September 10, not more than three laborers can be on vacation at the same time.
2. For the period September 11 through May 31, not more than two laborers can be on vacation at the same time.
3. The Director and the Foreman cannot be on vacation at the same time.
4. In cases where there are too many requests for the same vacation time than can be allowed by the above rules, the requests of those with the greater seniority will be granted.
5. In determining seniority, assume that all employees have continuous service from the date appointed.
6. No employee may take more leave days than the number of annual leave days he will accumulate through April 30. See the appropriate column in the table.
7. All vacation periods shown in the table begin on a Monday at 8 A.M. and end on a Friday at 5:00 P.M.
8. Employees work five days a week, Monday through Friday. They are off weekends and holidays with no changes to leave balances.
9. Holidays:

May 29	October 23	January 1
July 4	November 7	February 12
September 4	November 23	February 19
October 9	December 25	

10. An employee must take any part of his requests that is permissible under the above rules. If an employee is denied any part of his requests because of the above rules, he CANNOT change his requests.

18. The TOTAL number of annual leave days that will be charged to Williams for vacation is _____ days. 18.____
    A. 23 B. 24 C. 25 D. 26

19. The vacation dates that will be APPROVED for Mullen are 19.____
    A. June 26–August 4 only
    B. June 26–August 4; November 6-10
    C. November 6-10 only
    D. June 26-July 14; July 21-August 4

20. Reyes will be allowed to take _____ of his October vacation and _____ of his February vacation. 20.____
    A. all; all B. none; none C. some; all D. all; some

21. During how many months will there be NO ONE on vacation? 21.____
    A. 1 month B. 2 months C. 3 months D. 4 months

22. The vacation dates that will be APPROVED for Jones are 22.____
    A. July 31-September 1 only
    B. June 5-23; July 31-September 1
    C. June 5-23; July 31-August 18
    D. June 19-23; July 31-September 1

23. Which one of the following is the MOST accurate statement about Phillips' vacation requests? 23.____
    His requests
    A. *can* be granted in full because only one other laborer will be on vacation during the periods he requested
    B. *cannot* be granted in full because too many laborers with more seniority have requested some of the same time
    C. *can* be granted in full because he has more seniority than most of the other laborers
    D. *cannot* be granted in full because he will not have enough accumulated annual leave days through April 30, 2023

24. The vacation dates that will be approved for Ortiz are 24.____
    A. July 24-August 11; October 16-20
    B. July 24-August 11 only
    C. July 13-August 11; October 16-20
    D. October 16-20 only

25. The TOTAL number of annual leave days that will be charged to Spencer for his November vacation is _____ days. 25.____
    A. 10 B. 13 C. 14 D. 15

KEY (CORRECT ANSWERS)

1.	B	11.	A
2.	C	12.	B
3.	C	13.	C
4.	D	14.	B
5.	B	15.	B
6.	B	16.	A
7.	C	17.	D
8.	C	18.	B
9.	D	19.	A
10.	B	20.	C

21. B
22. D
23. D
24. A
25. B

TEST 4

DIRECTIONS: Each question or incomplete statement is followed by several suggested answers or completions. Select the one that BEST answers the question or completes the statement. *PRINT THE LETTER OF THE CORRECT ANSWER IN THE SPACE AT THE RIGHT.*

1. Suppose you, a foreman, receive a complaint over the telephone from a resident of the section. The complaint SHOULD be considered 1.____
   A. a matter which must be followed up
   B. a matter which will be followed up if the complaint is repeated
   C. evidence of poor functioning of the section
   D. unfounded until proved otherwise

2. The PROPER method for a foreman to answer the telephone in a section would be: 2.____
   A. "Hello, Department of _____"
   B. "Section 54, Foreman Jones"
   C. "Who is calling, please"
   D. "Whom do you wish to speak to"

3. Suppose that an applicant for a job as snow laborer presents to you, a foreman, a letter from a former employee stating, "John Smith has a pleasing manner and never got into an argument with his fellow employees. He was never late or absent. 3.____
   This letter
   A. indicates that, with some training, Smith will make a good snow gang boss
   B. presents no definite evidence of Smith's ability to do snow work
   C. proves definitely that Smith has never done any snow work before
   D. shows clearly that Smith will do better than average work as a snow laborer

4. When you step into a position that requires you to supervise others, you no longer do a great many specific jobs yourself; you direct your efforts toward getting others to do them. Instead of working with tools and machines, you are working with people. 4.____
   From this statement only, it follows that
   A. a foreman is not responsible for tools and machines
   B. a foreman should be able to do a great many specific jobs
   C. men are no different from tools and machines because each is required to do a specific job
   D. much of your success as a foreman will depend upon you ability to handle men

5. When supervising a worker, you should be 5.____
   A. fair in your actions towards him
   B. stern and to the point at all times
   C. apologetic and condescending
   D. sarcastic and smart

6. Assume that a worker under your supervision disagrees with your evaluation of his work. 6.____
Of the following statements, the one which describes the BEST way to handle the situation is to
   A. refuse to discuss his contention in order to maintain discipline
   B. advise him that the other men are satisfied with your evaluation and he has no right to complain
   C. explain to him that, since you have more working experience, you are more able to evaluate his work than he is
   D. explain the basis of your evaluation and discuss it with him

7. The MAIN responsibility of anyone who has men working under him is to 7.____
   A. make himself liked and respected by his men
   B. see that all his men are treated the same when duties are assigned
   C. create an attitude in his men which will be receptive toward policies of the department
   D. get the work done properly

8. The BEST way of giving directions to a worker is to 8.____
   A. lay out a rough plan of procedure and see whether the worker has the intelligence to work out his own method
   B. give only general hints of how you want the work accomplished
   C. be exact and omit none of the essential points
   D. question the helper frequently to determine whether he thinks that you have given him sufficient information

9. Following are four duties which are often described as "line" or "staff" functions performed by employees in an organization: 9.____
   I. Directing the efforts of a group of employees
   II. Observing work activities of employees and making appropriate reports
   III. Serving as technical specialist in a special project
   IV. Issuing orders to carry out a daily collection schedule

   The MOST appropriate way to label the four functions above is
   A. I and IV as "line" functions, and II and III as "staff" functions
   B. II and III as "line" functions, and I and IV as "staff" functions
   C. I, II, and IV as "line" functions and III as a "staff" function
   D. II and IV as "line" functions, and I and III as "staff" functions

10. For training purposes, it is generally considered that the MAXIMUM number of participants in a small-group discussion, for its maximum effectiveness, should be no more than 10.____
   A. 3 B. 6 C. 10 D. 15

KEY (CORRECT ANSWERS)

1.	A	6.	D
2.	B	7.	D
3.	B	8.	C
4.	D	9.	A
5.	A	10.	B

EXAMINATION SECTION

TEST 1

DIRECTIONS: Each question or incomplete statement is followed by several suggested answers or completions. Select the one that BEST answers the question or completes the statement. *PRINT THE LETTER OF THE CORRECT ANSWER IN THE SPACE AT THE RIGHT.*

1. Professional staff members in large organizations are sometimes frustrated by a lack of vital work-related information because of the failure of some middle-management supervisors to pass along unrestricted information from top management. 1.____
All of the following are considered to be reasons for such failure to pass along information EXCEPT the supervisors'
   A. belief that information affecting procedures will be ignored unless they are present to supervise their subordinates
   B. fear that specific information will require explanation or justification
   C. inclination to regard the possession of information as a symbol of higher status
   D. tendency to treat information a private property

2. Increasingly in government, employees' records are being handled by automated data processing systems. However, employees frequently doubt a computer's ability to handle their records properly. 2.____
Which of the following is the BEST way for management to overcome such doubts?
   A. Conduct a public relations campaign to explain the savings certain to result from the use of computers
   B. Use automated data processing equipment made by the firm which has the best repair facilities in the industry
   C. Maintain a clerical force to spot check on the accuracy of the computer's recordkeeping
   D. Establish automated data processing systems that are objective, impartial, and take into account individual factors as far as possible

3. Some management experts question the usefulness of offering cash to individual employees for their suggestions. 3.____
Which of the following reasons for opposing cash awards is MOST valid?
   A. Emphasis on individual gain deters cooperative effort.
   B. Money spent on evaluating suggestions may outweigh the value of the suggestions.
   C. Awards encourage employees to think about unusual methods of doing work.
   D. Suggestions too technical for ordinary evaluation are usually presented.

4. The use of outside consultants, rather than regular staff, in studying and recommending improvements in the operations of public agencies has been criticized. 4.____
Of the following, the BEST argument in favor of using regular staff is that such staff can better perform the work because they
   A. are more knowledgeable about operations and problems
   B. can more easily be organized into teams consisting of technical specialists
   C. may wish to gain additional professional experience
   D. will provide reports which will be more interesting to the public since they are more experienced

5. One approach to organizational problem-solving is to have all problem-solving authority centralized at the top of the organization. 5.____
However, from the viewpoint of providing maximum service to the public, this practice is UNWISE chiefly because it
   A. reduces the responsibility of the decision-makers
   B. produces delays
   C. reduces internal communications
   D. requires specialists

6. Research has shown that problem-solving efficiency is optimal when the motivation of the problem-solver is at a moderate rather than an extreme level. 6.____
Of the following, probably the CHIEF reason for this is that the problem-solver
   A. will cause confusion among his subordinates when his motivation is too high
   B. must avoid alternate solutions that tend to lead him up blind alleys
   C. can devote his attention to both the immediate problem as well as to other relevant problems in the general area
   D. must feel the need to solve the problem but not so urgently as to direct all his attention to the need and none to the means of solution

7. Don't be afraid to make mistakes. Many organizations are paralyzed from the fear of making mistakes. As a result, they don't do the things they should; they don't try new and different ideas. 7.____
For the effective supervisor, the MOST valid implication of this statement is that
   A. mistakes should not be encouraged, but there are some unavoidable risks in decision-making
   B. mistakes which stem from trying new and different ideas are usually not serious
   C. the possibility of doing things wrong is limited by one's organizational position
   D. the fear of making mistakes will prevent future errors

8. The duties of an employee under your supervision may be either routine, problem-solving, innovative, or creative. 8.____
Which of the following BEST describes duties which are both innovative and creative?

A. Checking to make sure that work is done properly
B. Applying principles in a practical matter
C. Developing new and better methods of meeting goals
D. Working at two or more jobs at the same time

9. According to modern management theory, a supervisor who uses as little authority as possible and as much as is necessary would be considered to be using a mode that is 9.____
A. autocratic B. inappropriate
C. participative D. directive

10. Delegation involves establishing and maintaining effective working arrangements between a supervisor and the persons who report to him. 10.____
Delegation is MOST likely to have taken place when the
A. entire staff openly discusses common problems in order to reach solutions satisfactory to the supervisor
B. performance of specified work is entrusted to a capable person, and the expected results are mutually understood
C. persons assigned to properly accomplish work are carefully evaluated and given a chance to explain shortcomings
D. supervisor provides specific written instructions in order to prevent anxiety on the part of inexperienced persons

11. Supervisors often not aware of the effect that their behavior has on their subordinates. 11.____
The one of the following training methods which would be BEST for changing such supervisory behavior is _____ training.
A. essential skills B. off-the-job
C. sensitivity D. developmental

12. A supervisor, in his role as a trainer, may have to decide on the length and frequency of training sessions. 12.____
When the material to be taught is new, difficult, and lengthy, the trainer should be guided by the principle that for BEST results in such circumstances, sessions should be
A. longer, relatively fewer in number, and held on successive days
B. shorter, relatively greater in number, and spaced at intervals of several days
C. of average length, relatively fewer in number, and held at intermittent intervals
D. of random length and frequency, but spaced at fixed intervals

13. Employee training which is based on realistic simulation, sometimes known as *game play* or *role play*, is sometimes preferable to learning from actual experience on the job. 13.____
Which of the following is NOT a correct statement concerning the value of simulation to trainees?

A. Simulation allows for practice in decision-making without any need for subsequent discussion.
B. Simulation is intrinsically motivating because it offers a variety of challenges.
C. Compared to other, more traditional training techniques, simulation is dynamic.
D. The simulation environment is nonpunitive as compared to real life.

14. Programmed instruction as a method of training has all of the following advantages EXCEPT: 14.____
A. Learning is accomplished in an optimum sequence of distinct steps.
B. Trainees have wide latitude in deciding what is to be learned within each program.
C. The trainee takes an active part in the learning process.
D. The trainee receives immediate knowledge of the results of his response.

15. In a work-study program, trainees were required to submit weekly written performance reports in order to insure that work assignments fulfilled the program objectives. 15.____
Such reports would also assist the administrator of the work-study program PRIMARILY to
A. eliminate personal counseling for the trainees
B. identify problems requiring prompt resolution
C. reduce the amount of clerical work for all concerned
D. estimate the rate at which budgeted funds are being expended

16. Which of the following would be MOST useful in order to avoid misunderstanding when preparing correspondence or reports? 16.____
A. Use vocabulary which is at an elementary level
B. Present each sentence as an individual paragraph
C. Have someone other than the writer read the material for clarity
D. Use general words which are open to interpretation

17. Which of the following supervisory methods would be MOST likely to train subordinates to give a prompt response to memoranda in an organizational setting where most transactions are informal? 17.____
A. Issue a written directive setting forth a schedule of strict deadlines
B. Let it be known, informally, that those who respond promptly will be rewarded
C. Follow up each memorandum by a personal inquiry regarding the receiver's reaction to it
D. Direct subordinates to furnish a precise explanation for ignoring memos

18. Conferences may fail for a number of reasons. Still, a conference that is an apparent failure may have some benefit. 18.____
Which of the following would LEAST likely be such a benefit?
It may
A. increase for most participants their possessiveness about information they have

B. produce a climate of good will and trust among many of the participants
C. provide most participants with an opportunity to learn things about the others
D. serve as a unifying force to keep most of the individuals functioning as a group

19. Assume that you have been assigned to study and suggest improvements in an operating unit of a delegate agency whose staff has become overwhelmed with problems, has had inadequate resources, and has become accustomed to things getting worse. The staff is indifferent to cooperating with you because they see no hope of improvement. 19.____
Which of the following steps would be LEAST useful in carrying out your assignment?
A. Encourage the entire staff to make suggestions to you for change
B. Inform the staff that management is somewhat dissatisfied with their performance
C. Let staff know that you are fully aware of their problems and stresses
D. Look for those problem area where changes can be made quickly

20. Which of the following statements about employer-employee relations is NOT considered to be correct by leading managerial experts? 20.____
A. An important factor in good employer-employee relations is treating workers respectfully.
B. Employer-employee relations are profoundly influenced by the fundamentals of human nature.
C. Good employer-employee relations must stem from top management and reach downward.
D. Employee unions are usually a major obstacle to establishing good employer-employee relations.

21. In connection with labor relations, the term *management rights* GENERALLY refers to 21.____
A. a managerial review system in a grievance system
B. statutory prohibitions that bar monetary negotiations
C. the impact of collective bargaining on government
D. those subjects which management considers to be non-negotiable

22. Barriers may exist to the utilization of women in higher level positions. Some of these barriers are attitudinal in nature. 22.____
Which of the following is MOST clearly attitudinal in nature?
A. Advancement opportunities which are vertical in nature and thus require seniority
B. Experience which is inadequate or irrelevant to the needs of a dynamic and progressive organization
C. Inadequate means of early identification of employees with talent and potential for advancement
D. Lack of self-confidence on the part of some women concerning their ability to handle a higher position

23. Because a reader reacts to the meaning he associates with a word, we can neve be sure what emotional impact a word may carry or how it may affect our readers. 23.____
The MOST logical implication of this statement for employees who correspond with members of the public is that
    A. a writer should try to select a neutral word that will not bias his writing by its hidden emotional meaning
    B. simple language should be used in writing letters denying requests so that readers are not upset by the denial
    C. every writer should adopt a writing style which he finds natural and easy
    D. whenever there is doubt as to how a word is defined, the dictionary should be consulted

24. A public information program should be based on clear information about the nature of actual public knowledge and opinion. One way of learning about the views of the public is through the use of questionnaires. 24.____
Which of the following is of LEAST importance in designing a questionnaire?
    A. A respondent should be asked for his name and address.
    B. A respondent should be asked to choose from among several statements the one which expresses his views.
    C. Questions should ask for responses in a form suitable for processing.
    D. Questions should be stated in familiar language.

25. Assume that you have accepted an invitation to speak before an interested group about a problem. You have brought with you for distribution a number of booklets and other informational material. 25.____
Of the following, which would be the BEST way to use this material?
    A. Distribute it before you begin talking so that the audience may read it at their leisure.
    B. Distribute it during your talk to increase the likelihood that it will be read.
    C. Hold it until the end of your talk, then announce that those who wish may take or examine the material.
    D. Before starting the talk, leave it on a table in the back of the room so that people may pick it up as they enter.

KEY (CORRECT ANSWERS)

1.	A	11.	C
2.	D	12.	B
3.	A	13.	A
4.	A	14.	B
5.	B	15.	B
6.	D	16.	C
7.	A	17.	C
8.	C	18.	A
9.	C	19.	B
10.	B	20.	D

21. D
22. D
23. A
24. A
25. C

TEST 2

DIRECTIONS: Each question or incomplete statement is followed by several suggested answers or completions. Select the one that BEST answers the question or completes the statement. *PRINT THE LETTER OF THE CORRECT ANSWER IN THE SPACE AT THE RIGHT.*

1. Of the following, the FIRST step in planning an operation is to 1.____
   A. obtain relevant information
   B. identify the goal to be achieved
   C. consider possible alternatives
   D. make necessary assignments

2. A supervisor who is extremely busy performing routine tasks is MOST likely making INCORRECT use of what basic principle of supervision? 2.____
   A. Homogeneous Assignment
   B. Span of Control
   C. Work Distribution
   D. Delegation of Authority

3. Controls help supervisors to obtain information from which they can determine whether their staffs are achieving planned goals. 3.____
   Which one of the following would be LEAST useful as a control device?
   A. Employee diaries
   B. Organization charts
   C. Periodic inspections
   D. Progress charts

4. A certain employee has difficulty in effectively performing a particular portion of his routine assignments, but his overall productivity is average. 4.____
   As the direct supervisor of his individual, your BEST course of action would be to
   A. attempt to develop the man's capacity to execute the problematic facets of his assignments
   B. diversify the employee's work assignments in order to build up his confidence
   C. reassign the man to less difficult tasks
   D. request in a private conversation that the employee improve his work output

5. A supervisor who uses persuasion as a means of supervising a unit would GENERALLY also use which of the following practices to supervise his unit? 5.____
   A. Supervise and control the staff with an authoritative attitude to indicate that he is a *take-charge* individual
   B. Make significant changes in the organizational operations so as to improve job efficiency
   C. Remove major communication barriers between himself, subordinates, and management
   D. Supervise everyday operations while being mindful of the problems of his subordinates

6. Whenever a supervisor in charge of a unit delegate a routine task to a capable subordinate, he tells him exactly how to do it. 6.____

This practice is GENERALLY
- A. *desirable*, chiefly because good supervisors should be aware of the traits of their subordinates and delegate responsibilities to them accordingly
- B. *undesirable*, chiefly because only non-routine tasks should be delegated
- C. *desirable*, chiefly because a supervisor should frequently test the willingness of his subordinates to perform ordinary tasks
- D. *undesirable*, chiefly because a capable subordinate should usually be allowed to exercise his own discretion in doing a routine job

7. The one of the following activities through which a supervisor BEST demonstrates leadership ability is by 7.____
   - A. arranging periodic staff meetings in order to keep his subordinates informed about professional developments in the field
   - B. frequently issuing definite orders and directives which will lessen the need for subordinates to make decisions in handling any tasks assigned to them
   - C. devoting the major part of his time to supervising subordinates so as to simulate continuous improvement
   - D. setting aside time for self-development and research so as to improve the skills, techniques, and procedures of his unit

8. The following three statements relate to the supervision of employees: 8.____
   - I. The assignment of difficult tasks that offer a challenge is more conducive to good morale than the assignment of easy tasks.
   - II. The same general principles of supervision that apply to men are equally applicable to women.
   - III. The best retraining program should cover all phases of an employee's work in a general manner.

   Which of the following choices list ALL of the above statements that are generally correct?

   A. II, III B. I C. I, II D. I, II, III

9. Which of the following examples BEST illustrates the application of the *exception principle* as a supervisory technique? 9.____
   - A. A complex job is divided among several employees who work simultaneously to complete the whole job in a shorter time.
   - B. An employee is required to complete any task delegated to him to such an extent that nothing is left for the superior who delegated the task except to approve it.
   - C. A superior delegates responsibility to a subordinate but retains authority to make the final decisions.
   - D. A superior delegates all work possible to his subordinates and retains that which requires his personal attention or performance

10. Assume that you are a supervisor. Your immediate superior frequently gives orders to your subordinates without your knowledge. 10.____

    Of the following, the MOST direct and effective way for you to handle this problem is to

A. tell our subordinates to take orders only from you
B. submit a report to higher authority in which you cite specific instances
C. discuss it with your immediate superior
D. find out to what extent your authority and prestige as a supervisor have been affected

11. In an agency which has as its primary purpose the protection of the public against fraudulent business practices, which of the following would GENERALLY be considered an *auxiliary* or *staff* rather than a *line* function? 11.____
A. Interviewing victims of frauds and advising them about their legal remedies
B. Daily activities directed toward prevention of fraudulent business practices
C. Keeping records and statistics about business violations reported and corrected
D. Follow-up inspections by investigators after corrective action has been taken

12. A supervisor can MOST effectively reduce the spread of false rumors through the *grapevine* by 12.____
A. identifying and disciplining any subordinate responsible for initiating such rumors
B. keeping his subordinates informed as much as possible about matters affecting them
C. denying false rumors which might tend to lower staff morale and productivity
D. making sure confidential matters are kept secure from access by unauthorized employees

13. A supervisor has tried to learn about the background, education, and family relationships of his subordinates through observation, personal contact, and inspection of their personnel records. 13.____
These supervisor actions are GENERALLY
A. *inadvisable*, chiefly because they may lead to charges of favoritism
B. *advisable*, chiefly because they may make him more popular with his subordinates
C. *inadvisable*, chiefly because his efforts may be regarded as an invasion of privacy
D. *advisable*, chiefly because the information may enable him to develop better understanding of each of his subordinates

14. In an emergency situation, when action must be taken immediately, it is BEST for the supervisor to give orders in the form of 14.____
A. direct commands which are brief and precise
B. requests, so that his subordinates will not become alarmed
C. suggestions which offer alternative courses of action
D. implied directives, so that his subordinates may use their judgment in carrying them out

15. When demonstrating a new and complex procedure to a group of subordinates, it is ESSENTIAL that a supervisor 15.____
    A. go slowly and repeat the steps involved at least once
    B. show the employees common errors and the consequences of such errors
    C. go through the process at the usual speed so that the employees can see the rate at which they should work
    D. distribute summaries of the procedure during the demonstration and instruct his subordinates to refer to them afterwards

16. After a procedures manual has been written and distributed, 16.____
    A. continuous maintenance work is necessary to keep the manual current
    B. it is best to issue new manuals rather than make changes in the original manual
    C. no changes should be necessary
    D. only major changes should be considered

17. Of the following, the MOST important criterion of effective report writing is 17.____
    A. eloquence of writing style
    B. the use of technical language
    C. to be brief and to the point
    D. to cover all details

18. The use of electronic data processing 18.____
    A. has proven unsuccessful in most organizations
    B. has unquestionable advantages for all organizations
    C. is unnecessary in most organizations
    D. should be decided upon only after careful feasibility studies by individual organizations

19. The PRIMARY purpose of work measurement is to 19.____
    A. design and install a wage incentive program
    B. determine who should be promoted
    C. establish a yardstick to determine extent of progress
    D. set up a spirit of competition among employee

20. The action which is MOST effective in gaining acceptance of a study by the agency which is being studied is 20.____
    A. a directive from the agency head to install a study based on recommendations included in a report
    B. a lecture-type presentation following approval of the procedure
    C. a written procedure in narrative form covering the proposed system with visual presentations and discussions
    D. procedural charts showing the *before* situation, forms, steps, etc., to the employees affected

21. Which organization principle is MOST closely related to procedural analysis and improvement? 21.____
    A. Duplication, overlapping, and conflict should be eliminated.
    B. Managerial authority should be clearly defined.
    C. The objectives of the organization should be clearly defined.
    D. Top management should be freed of burdensome detail.

22. Which one of the following is the MAJOR objective of operational audits? 22.____
    A. Detecting fraud
    B. Determining organization problems
    C. Determining the number of personnel needed
    D. Recommending opportunities for improving operating and management practices

23. Of the following, the formalization of organization structure is BEST achieved by 23.____
    A. a narrative description of the plan of organization
    B. functional charts
    C. job descriptions together with organization charts
    D. multi-flow charts

24. Budget planning is MOST useful when it achieves 24.____
    A. cost control
    B. forecast of receipts
    C. performance review
    D. personnel reduction

25. GENERALLY, in applying the principle of delegation in dealing with subordinates, a supervisor 25.____
    A. allows his subordinates to set up work goals and to fix the limits within which they can work
    B. allows his subordinates to set up work goals and then gives detailed orders as to how they are to be achieved
    C. makes relatively few decisions by himself and frames his orders in broad, general terms
    D. provides externalized motivation for his subordinate

KEY (CORRECT ANSWERS)

1. B
2. D
3. B
4. A
5. D

6. D
7. C
8. C
9. D
10. C

11. C
12. B
13. D
14. A
15. A

16. A
17. C
18. D
19. C
20. C

21. A
22. D
23. C
24. A
25. C

www.ingramcontent.com/pod-product-compliance
Lightning Source LLC
Chambersburg PA
CBHW081818300426
44116CB00014B/2405
* 9 7 8 1 7 9 9 3 6 7 0 3 1 *